First World War
and Army of Occupation
War Diary
France, Belgium and Germany

47 DIVISION
Headquarters, Branches and Services
General Staff
1 February 1915 - 30 April 1915

WO95/2696

The Naval & Military Press Ltd
www.nmarchive.com
Published in association with The National Archives

Published by

The Naval & Military Press Ltd

Unit 10 Ridgewood Industrial Park,

Uckfield, East Sussex,

TN22 5QE England

Tel: +44 (0) 1825 749494

www.naval-military-press.com

www.nmarchive.com

This diary has been reprinted in facsimile from the original. Any imperfections are inevitably reproduced and the quality may fall short of modern type and cartographic standards.

© Crown Copyright
Images reproduced by permission of The National Archives, London, England, 2015.

Contents

Document type	Place/Title	Date From	Date To
Heading	47th Division General Staff 1915 Feb-Apr		
War Diary	St. Albans	01/02/1915	27/02/1915
War Diary	St. Albans	05/02/1915	01/03/1915
Miscellaneous	War Diaries.	06/02/1915	06/02/1915
Miscellaneous	War Diary Statement.	07/02/1915	07/02/1915
Miscellaneous	Skeleton Form of War Diary.		
Miscellaneous	Training.		
Miscellaneous			
Miscellaneous	A Form Messages And Signals.		
Miscellaneous	Permits required to complete establishment		
Miscellaneous	1/6th London Infantry Brigade.	09/02/1915	09/02/1915
Miscellaneous	Skeleton Form of War Diary.		
Heading	General Staff 47th Div. March 1915		
Miscellaneous			
War Diary	St. Albans	01/03/1915	18/03/1915
War Diary	Marles Les Mines	22/03/1915	31/03/1915
War Diary	St Albans	02/03/1915	09/03/1915
Miscellaneous	Composition of 1/2nd London Division Booklet Dated 1st March 1915 S.D.2	04/03/1915	04/03/1915
Miscellaneous	Copy Telegram	02/03/1915	02/03/1915
Miscellaneous	1/4th Inf. Bdes		
Miscellaneous	C Form (Duplicate) Messages And Signals.		
Miscellaneous	Copy Telegram	03/03/1915	03/03/1915
Miscellaneous	K.E.H.	03/03/1915	03/03/1915
Miscellaneous	Headquarters, 1/6th London Infantry Brigade	03/03/1915	03/03/1915
Miscellaneous	Courses of Instruction		
Miscellaneous	A Form. Messages And Signals.		
Miscellaneous	Copy of Telegram	06/03/1915	06/03/1915
Miscellaneous	Secretary War Office London	07/03/1915	07/03/1915
Miscellaneous			
Miscellaneous	Centraforce Horse Guards London	07/03/1915	07/03/1915
Miscellaneous	120/General Number/7735 (Q.M.G.2.)	08/03/1915	08/03/1915
Miscellaneous	1/2nd London Division.		
Miscellaneous			
Miscellaneous	1/2nd London Division T.F. Distribution of Instructions.	09/03/1915	09/03/1915
Miscellaneous	From Brig. Gen J.C. Wray, M.V.O. Commanding Divisional Artillery, 1/2nd London Division, T.F.	09/03/1915	09/03/1915
Miscellaneous	The General Officer Commanding 3rd Army. Control Force.	10/03/1916	10/03/1916
Miscellaneous	The Secretary War Office London S.W.	14/03/1915	14/03/1915
Miscellaneous	Headquarters. 1st Army Corps.	19/03/1915	19/03/1915
Miscellaneous	1st Corps. Return of feeding strength for week ending	20/03/1915	20/03/1915
Operation(al) Order(s)	1st Corps Operation Order No. 75	21/03/1915	21/03/1915
Miscellaneous	Headquarters 1st Army Corps.	22/03/1915	22/03/1915
Miscellaneous	Report on Disembarkation to 2nd London Division.	23/03/1915	23/03/1915
Miscellaneous			
Miscellaneous	Not to be Written on		
Miscellaneous		23/03/1915	23/03/1915
Miscellaneous	Headquarters I.G.C.	26/03/1915	26/03/1915

Miscellaneous	Report on The Disembarkation of The 2nd London Territorial Division.	22/03/1915	22/03/1915
Miscellaneous	Record of Transport for 2nd London Division.		
Miscellaneous	Report on the Disembarkation and Entrainment of the 1/2nd. London. (territorial) Division.	23/03/1915	23/03/1915
Miscellaneous	Havre Base	19/03/1915	19/03/1915
Miscellaneous	Report on complaint by Lt-Col. Thwaites. C.S.O. 2nd London Division.	19/03/1915	19/03/1915
Miscellaneous	Type		
Miscellaneous	Havre Base		
Miscellaneous	Report on complaint by Lt-Col. Thwaites. C.S.O. 2nd London Division.	19/03/1915	19/03/1915
Miscellaneous	D.A.Q.M.G.	24/03/1915	24/03/1915
Miscellaneous	Embarkation Commandant Southampton	23/03/1915	23/03/1915
Miscellaneous			
Miscellaneous	Report on Disembarkation of 2nd London Division.	23/03/1915	23/03/1915
Miscellaneous	Schedule of Correspondence.	23/03/1915	23/03/1915
Miscellaneous	Report on The Disembarkation of The 2nd London Territorial Division.	22/03/1915	22/03/1915
Miscellaneous	Record of Transport for 2nd London Division.		
Miscellaneous	Report on The Disembarkation of The 2nd London Territorial Division.	22/03/1915	22/03/1915
Miscellaneous	Record of Transport for 2nd London Division.		
Miscellaneous	Report on The Disembarkation of The 2nd London Territorial Division.	22/03/1915	22/03/1915
Miscellaneous	Record of Transport for 2nd London Division.		
Miscellaneous	Report on in Disembarkation of The 2nd London Territorial Division	22/03/1915	22/03/1915
Miscellaneous	Not to be Written on.		
Miscellaneous	C Form (Original). Messages And Signals.		
Miscellaneous	A Form. Messages And Signals.		
Miscellaneous	A Form. Messages And Signals.	24/03/1915	24/03/1915
Miscellaneous	2nd London Division.	24/03/1915	24/03/1915
Miscellaneous	2nd London Division	24/03/1915	24/03/1915
Miscellaneous	Headquarters 2nd London Division.	24/03/1915	24/03/1915
Miscellaneous	Lt Col Division.	26/03/1915	26/03/1915
Miscellaneous	4th (Guards) Brigade.	25/03/1915	25/03/1915
Miscellaneous	A Form. Messages And Signals.		
Miscellaneous	1st Corps Hqrs	27/03/1915	27/03/1915
Miscellaneous	A Form. Messages And Signals.		
Miscellaneous			
Miscellaneous	A Form. Messages And Signals.		
Miscellaneous	Officer Commanding 2nd Lon. Div. Cyclist Compy.	28/03/1915	28/03/1915
Miscellaneous	A Form. Messages And Signals.		
Miscellaneous	C Form (Duplicate) Messages And Signals.		
Miscellaneous	2nd London Division T.F. Billeting Areas on March 27th.		
Miscellaneous	Report on Work of 2nd London Division Battalions Attached to 2nd Division.	28/03/1915	28/03/1915
Miscellaneous	Headquarters 2nd London Division.	29/03/1915	29/03/1915
Miscellaneous	2nd London Division.	29/03/1915	29/03/1915
Miscellaneous	2nd London Division.	30/03/1915	30/03/1915
Miscellaneous	4th Hon. Inf. Bde.	31/03/1915	31/03/1915
Miscellaneous	Instruction of Territorial Battalions.	01/04/1915	01/04/1915
Miscellaneous	Head Quarter 2nd Lon Division.	01/04/1915	01/04/1915
Miscellaneous	A Form. Messages And Signals.		

Miscellaneous	C Form (Duplicate) Messages And Signals.		
Miscellaneous	A Form Messages And Signals.		
Miscellaneous	2nd London Division.	29/03/1915	29/03/1915
Miscellaneous	A Form Messages And Signals.		
Miscellaneous	C Form (Duplicate) Messages And Signals.		
Miscellaneous	A Form. Messages And Signals.		
Miscellaneous	C Form (Duplicate) Messages And Signals.		
Miscellaneous	A Form Messages And Signals.		
Miscellaneous	C Form (Duplicate). Messages And Signals.		
Miscellaneous	A Form. Messages And Signals.		
Miscellaneous	C Form (Duplicate) Messages And Signals.		
Miscellaneous	A Form. Messages And Signals.		
Miscellaneous	C Form (Duplicate) Messages And Signals.		
Miscellaneous	A Form. Messages And Signals.		
Miscellaneous	C Form (Duplicate) Messages And Signals.		
Miscellaneous			
Miscellaneous	A Form Messages And Signals.		
Miscellaneous	Instructions of 6th, 7th, 8th, London Battalion.	30/03/1915	30/03/1915
Miscellaneous	Headquarters 2nd Lon Div	03/04/1915	03/04/1915
Miscellaneous	A Form. Messages And Signals.		
Heading	War Diary 47th Div. General Staff April 1915		
Miscellaneous	81th Brigade Appendix to War Diary Vol. IV		
Miscellaneous	London Divn War Diary (G.S.) Attached		
War Diary	Marles Les Mines.	01/04/1915	17/04/1915
War Diary	Mensecq	18/04/1915	19/04/1915
War Diary	Chateau Philomel Mensecq	20/04/1915	20/04/1915
War Diary	Mensecq	21/04/1915	24/04/1915
War Diary	Bethune	25/04/1915	25/04/1915
Miscellaneous	Occupation of Trench Line.		
War Diary		25/04/1915	25/04/1915
War Diary	Bethune	26/04/1915	30/04/1915
Miscellaneous	Casualties-25th March to 30th April 1915	25/03/1915	25/03/1915
Map	London Division Positions in Front Line April 1915		
Miscellaneous	A Form. Messages And Signals		
Miscellaneous			
Miscellaneous	2nd London Division.	01/04/1915	01/04/1915
Miscellaneous	1/2nd London Division.	01/04/1915	01/04/1915
Miscellaneous	Instruction of Territorial Battalions.	01/04/1915	01/04/1915
Miscellaneous	Headquarters 2nd London Division	02/04/1915	02/04/1915
Miscellaneous		01/03/1915	01/03/1915
Miscellaneous	Headquarters 1st Division.	02/04/1915	02/04/1915
Miscellaneous	Headquarters, 6th London Infantry Brigade.	02/04/1915	02/04/1915
Miscellaneous	Headquarters, 5th Lon. Inf. Brigade.	02/04/1915	02/04/1915
Miscellaneous	1st Corps No. 251 (G).	02/04/1915	02/04/1915
Miscellaneous	A Form. Messages And Signals.		
Miscellaneous			
Miscellaneous	Instruction of Territorial Battalions.	03/04/1915	03/04/1915
Miscellaneous	Headquarters 2nd London Division.	04/04/1915	04/04/1915
Miscellaneous	Headquarters 2nd. Lon Division.		
Miscellaneous	A Form. Messages And Signals.		
Miscellaneous	2nd London Division.	04/04/1915	04/04/1915
Miscellaneous	Headquarters 2nd London Division.	06/04/1915	06/04/1915
Miscellaneous	A Form. Messages And Signals.		
Miscellaneous	2nd London Division.	05/04/1915	05/04/1915
Miscellaneous	Headquarters 2nd London Division.		
Operation(al) Order(s)	1st Division Order No. 76	05/04/1915	05/04/1915

Miscellaneous	6th Lon. Inf. Bde.	06/04/1915	06/04/1915
Map	Issued with first-Corps Operation Order No 76		
Miscellaneous	6th Lon. Inf. Bde.	08/04/1915	08/04/1915
Miscellaneous	A Form. Messages And Signals.		
Miscellaneous	1st Division.		
Miscellaneous			
Miscellaneous	A Form. Messages And Signals.		
Miscellaneous	1st Corps. No. 289. (C)	07/04/1915	07/04/1915
Miscellaneous		07/04/1915	07/04/1915
Miscellaneous	6th Lon. Inf. Bde.	08/04/1915	08/04/1915
Miscellaneous			
Operation(al) Order(s)	First Corps Operation Order No. 76	08/04/1915	08/04/1915
Miscellaneous	Instruction Territorial Battalions.	08/04/1915	08/04/1915
Miscellaneous	2nd London Division.	10/04/1915	10/04/1915
Miscellaneous	Instruction of Territorial Battalions.	11/04/1915	11/04/1915
Miscellaneous	2nd London Division.	12/04/1915	12/04/1915
Miscellaneous	2nd London Div.	13/04/1915	13/04/1915
Miscellaneous	G.O.C. 2nd London Div.	13/04/1915	13/04/1915
Miscellaneous	Paper "A" General Instructions For The Attack.		
Miscellaneous	Paper "B" General Principles For The Attack		
Miscellaneous	Instruction of Territorial Battalions.	14/04/1915	14/04/1915
Miscellaneous	Report on 15th Civil Service.	16/04/1915	16/04/1915
Miscellaneous	Report on 17th London Territorial Battalion.	16/04/1915	16/04/1915
Miscellaneous	Instruction of Territorial Battalions.	15/04/1915	15/04/1915
Miscellaneous	Suggested plan for Move of Battalion of 2nd London Division to 2nd Division Area. 18th and 19th April.	18/04/1915	18/04/1915
Miscellaneous	1st Guards Brigade	18/04/1915	18/04/1915
Miscellaneous	1st Guards Brigade		
Miscellaneous	6th Bde. No. 495	17/04/1915	17/04/1915
Miscellaneous	1st Corps No. 289 (G)	18/04/1915	18/04/1915
Miscellaneous	1st Corps Draft Operation Order.		
Miscellaneous	Notes for 1st Corps Conference.	20/04/1915	20/04/1915
Miscellaneous	Notes London Div. Conference	21/04/1915	21/04/1915
Operation(al) Order(s)	1st Corps Operation Order No. 77	20/04/1915	20/04/1915
Miscellaneous	1st Corps Instructions	29/04/1915	29/04/1915
Miscellaneous	1st Brigade.	21/04/1915	21/04/1915
Operation(al) Order(s)	1st Corps Operation Order No. 78	23/04/1915	23/04/1915
Miscellaneous	C Form (Duplicate) Messages And Signals		
Operation(al) Order(s)	London Division Operation Order No. 1	23/04/1915	23/04/1915
Miscellaneous	4th Lon. Inf. Bde.	23/04/1915	23/04/1915
Miscellaneous	1st Corps.	22/04/1915	22/04/1915
Miscellaneous	4th Lon. Inf. Bde.	23/04/1915	23/04/1915
Miscellaneous	1st Corps No. 251 (G).	22/04/1915	22/04/1915
Miscellaneous	A Form. Messages And Signals.		
Miscellaneous	Special Instructions to Artillery.	24/04/1915	24/04/1915
Miscellaneous	London Division.	24/04/1915	24/04/1915
Miscellaneous	1st Divn. No. 201 (G).	22/04/1915	24/04/1915
Miscellaneous	1st Corps Instructions. (2).	25/04/1915	25/04/1915
Miscellaneous	A Form. Messages And Signals.		
Miscellaneous	C Form (Duplicate) Messages And Signals		
Miscellaneous	London Division Appendices to War Diary (G.S) April 25th-26th	25/04/1915	25/04/1915
Miscellaneous	A Form. Messages And Signals.		
Miscellaneous		26/04/1915	26/04/1915
Miscellaneous	Tactical Progress Report of London Division up to Noon 25th April, 1915	25/04/1915	25/04/1915

Miscellaneous	Amendments to-Lon. Div. Secret Memo No. G/111, dated 26th April, 1915	26/04/1915	26/04/1915
Miscellaneous	Headquarters 1st Corps.	26/04/1915	26/04/1915
Miscellaneous	Principles for Defence of Festubert and Rue De L'Epinette ("C" and "D.1") Sections, and eventually to include Givenchy and Cuinchy ("B" and "A") Sections.	26/04/1915	26/04/1915
Miscellaneous	A Form. Messages And Signals.		
Miscellaneous	C Form (Duplicate) Messages And Signals		
Miscellaneous	A Form. Messages And Signals.		
Miscellaneous	Tactical Progress Report of London Division. up to Noon 26th April, 1915	26/04/1915	26/04/1915
Miscellaneous	Principles for Defence of Festubert and Rue De L'Epinette ("C" and "D.1") Sections, and eventually to include Givenchy and Cuinchy ("B" and "A") Sections.	26/04/1915	26/04/1915
Miscellaneous	Tactical Progress Report of London Division. up to Noon, 27th April 1915	27/04/1915	27/04/1915
Miscellaneous	Appendices to War Diary London Divn. (General Staff) April 27th-30th	27/04/1915	27/04/1915
Miscellaneous	A Form. Messages And Signals.		
Miscellaneous	C Form (Duplicate) Messages And Signals		
Miscellaneous	A Form. Messages And Signals.		
Miscellaneous	C Form (Duplicate) Messages And Signals		
Miscellaneous	O.C. 23rd Bde.	28/04/1915	28/04/1915
Miscellaneous	Headquarters. London Division.	28/04/1915	28/04/1915
Miscellaneous	H.Q. London Division	28/04/1915	28/04/1915
Miscellaneous	Amendments to Lon. Div. Secret Memo No. G/111, dated 26th April, 1915	26/04/1915	26/04/1915
Miscellaneous	Tactical Progress Report of London Division. up to Noon 28th April, 1918	28/04/1918	28/04/1918
Miscellaneous	A Form. Messages And Signals.		
Miscellaneous	2nd. London Division. Billets Occupied By Units on Night of 29th. April, 1915	29/04/1915	29/04/1915
Miscellaneous	Tactical Progress Report of London Division up to Noon 29th April 1915	29/04/1915	29/04/1915
Miscellaneous	Headquarters London Division.	29/04/1915	29/04/1915
Miscellaneous	6th Lon. Inf. Bde.	30/04/1915	30/04/1915
Miscellaneous	Conference, 1st Army 27th April At Bethune	30/04/1915	30/04/1915
Miscellaneous	A Form. Messages And Signals.		
Miscellaneous	C Form (Duplicate) Messages And Signals.		
Miscellaneous	A Form. Messages And Signals		
Miscellaneous	C Form (Duplicate) Messages And Signals.		
Miscellaneous	A Form. Messages And Signals.		
Miscellaneous	Tactical Progress Report of London Division. up to noon 30th April 1915	30/04/1915	30/04/1915

47TH DIVISION

GENERAL STAFF
MAR — APR 1915

1915 FEB — APR

Army Form C. 2118.

WAR DIARY
or
INTELLIGENCE SUMMARY
(Erase heading not required.)

Instructions regarding War Diaries and Intelligence Summaries are contained in F. S. Regs., Part II. and the Staff Manual respectively. Title pages will be prepared in manuscript.

Hour, Date, Place	Summary of Events and Information	Remarks and references to Appendices
February, 1915. ST. ALBANS.		
Feb. 1st.	Divisional Concentration march for inspection by Sir A. Codrington.	
Feb. 3rd.	Divisional exercise without troops.	
Feb. 4th.	Ditto.	
Feb. 9th.	One Officer and two N. C. O's proceed to Bisley for machine gun course. First Brigade-School of musketry under Officers and N.C.O's from BISLEY assembles.	
Feb. 10th.	2nd. Lieut. Corby 1/21st. Battn. proceeds to Hythe for course of instruction in one-man range finder.	
Feb. 12th.	Divisional Exercise.	
Feb. 15th.	20 men attached to R. F. A. for instruction in ride and drive. Battalion Signal Sections struck off all duties for instruction in Morse (small flag and buzzer.)	
Feb. 16th.	1/21st Battn. moves from LUTON to HARPENDEN.	
Feb. 18th.	Lecture by Lt. Col. Thwaites on "The German Army".	
Feb. 21st.	Three men attached to A. S. C. for instruction in cold shoeing.	
Feb. 22nd.	Divisional Exercise.	
Feb. 24th.	Second Brigade School of musketry assembles.	
Feb. 25th.	One Officer and One N. C. O. proceed to Bisley for machine gun course.	
Feb. 26th.	Divisional Infantry Operations.	
Feb. 27th.	Draft of 54 N.C.O's and men arrive from reserve battalion 1/23rd Bn. The London Regiment.	

Brigadier General comdg.
1/6th. London Infty. Bde.

Mar. 10th., 1915.

A.F. C.2118.

WAR DIARY.

Hour, date, place.	Summary of events & information	Remarks & references to Appendices.
ST ALBANS.		
5/2/1915	Company training.	
6/2/1915	Company training.	
7/2/1915	Night march.	
8/2/1915	Battalion training.	
9/2/1915	" "	
10/2/1915	Company training.	
11/2/1915	Brigade Class of Instruction for N.C.Os.	
12/2/1915	Company training.	
13/2/1915	Battalion training.	
15/2/1915 (afternoon)	Class for N.C.Os in use of compass, &c.	
	Divisional Exercise.	
	Wood fighting.	
	Recruits Musketry	Part II, Table B, Appendix 4.
16/2/1915	Coy. training in Gorhambury Park.	
	Trained men's training.	
	Officers' revolver practice.	Part III, Table B, Appendix I.
17/2/1915	Trained men's Musketry.	Part III, Table B, Appendix 1.
18/2/1915	" "	---do---
19/2/1915	Company training.	
	Trained men's Musketry.	
	Officers' revolver practice.	
20/2/1915	Musketry.	
22/2/1915	Divisional Exercise.	
23/2/1915	Battalion Concentration march.	
24/2/1915	Route march.	
25/2/1915	Concentration march.	
26/2/1915	Inter-Brigade Exercise.	
27/2/1915	Company training.	
	1 Officer & 1 N.C.O. attending Hand-grenade throwing at Radlett.	
	Draft of 54 N.C.Os and men arrived from Reserve Battalion.	
1/3/1915	Route march.	

WAR DIARIES.

Unit: 1/23rd Battalion The London Regiment.

Brigade: 1/6th London Infantry Brigade.

Division: 1/2nd London Division, Territorial Force.

Mobilization Centre: 27, St John's Hill, Clapham Junction, S.W.

Temporary War Station: ST ALBANS.

-o-o-o-o-o-o-o-o-o-o-o-o-

(D) TRAINING.   I have little to add to my remarks of last month. The re-formation of a Battalion into four Companies instead of eight has made it necessary to have a lot of steady Company and Platoon Drill. This is making good progress, and I consider that this new formation is more convenient for training a Territorial battalion than the old one.

A certain amount of night work has also been performed.

(E) MUSKETRY. The field firing of the Battalion has been completed; otherwise there has not been much progress in Musketry, owing to the range not having been available.   The Miniature range has been freely used, both by Trained Men and Recruits.

(E) DISCIPLINE.   There is nothing to add to my last report. The Platoon formation seems to have brought out many good points in the non-commissioned-officers: they seem much more ready to accept responsibility than formerly.

[signature]

Lieut. Colonel,

Commanding, 1/23rd Battn. The London Regt.

ST ALBANS
6/2/15.

WAR DIARY STATEMENT.
....

22nd Bn LONDON REGT (THE QUEEN'S).
6th LONDON INFANTRY BRIGADE.
2nd LONDON DIVISION.

MOBILIZATION CENTRE ---------------------------BERMONDSEY

WAR STATION -------------------------------------ST ALBANS.

(1) TRAINING.

    (a) FIELD OPERATIONS -- No remarks.

    (b) MUSKETRY. A special report will be forwarded on this subject when the Musketry Returns have been compiled.

                                      Lieut-Col
                Comdg 22nd Bn LONDON REGT (QUEEN'S).

St Albans.
    7/2/15.

SKELETON FORM OF WAR DIARY.

Unit..........................

Brigade........................

Division........................

Mobilization Centre............

Temporary War Station..........

Stations since occupied subsequent to concentration.............
....

(a) MOBILIZATION.

(b) CONCENTRATION AT WAR STATIONS (including Railway Moves)

(c) ORGANIZATION FOR DEFENCE (including vulnerable points)

(d) TRAINING.

(e) DISCIPLINE.

(f) ADMINISTRATION.

    1. Medical services.

    2. Veterinary services.

    3. Supply Services.

    4. Transport Services.

    5. Ordnance Services.

    6. Billetting and Hutting.

    7. Channels of correspondence in routine matters.

    8. Range construction.

    9. Supply of Remounts.

(g) REORGANIZATION OF T.F. INTO HOME AND IMPERIAL SERVICE.

(h) PREPARATION OF UNITS FOR IMPERIAL SERVICE.

(a) ...
(b) ...
(c) ...

Training.

The 4 Company system was introduced at the commencement of the month, and Company Drill and training has been carried out. An improvement has been shown in the work of the junior commissioned ranks and NCO's, as a result of the platoon system which has increased their responsibility.
Digging by day and night has been practised.
Judging Distance tests were carried out. The results are not very satisfactory.
Col. 2i/c has inspected all the units in the Bde. in marching order on different days.

Machine Gun Sections were concentrated at Hatfield and School of Instruction for training of 2 extra sections per unit commenced.
The organisation of the training & work by the Brigade Machine Gun officer have been thoroughly efficient. The exact position to fill is urgently required.

Musketry.

During the month the 21st & 22nd Bns completed the course prescribed by 3rd A.O. No. — at Cockenbury & the 23rd & 24th Bns have fired the same course at Warden Hill & Hatfield respectively. As the Bns completed the Field firing part of the course at Dunstable during the week ending 30th Jan.
The results showed a marked improvement in the tactical handling & fire control of the men.

Pondicherry may perhaps be one the whole marked by a variety of the different suits of the Ave.

(E) Description continues to be very good.

E. Administration

(1) (2) (3) Satisfactory.

(4) Transport Service. Still in process of reorganisation. The drivers from each unit have been attached for instruction to R.A.

(5) Ordnance Services —
The scarcity of dummy cartridges still continues.

(6) Billeting and Hutting. The 21st & 24th have been able to obtain more satisfactory accommodation for their horses at Sutton & Hatfield respectively.
The accommodation for horses in the billeting area of the 23rd Bat'n is very scattered & unsatisfactory.

(7) Nil.

(8) The 24th Bat'n have taken over an additional musketry range at Hatfield which is now up to date and satisfactory.

G. Nil

H. No recruits have been received.
Establishments?

"A" Form. Army Form C. 2121.

MESSAGES AND SIGNALS.

To go at end of training report:

Classes of instron in the French language are being held every afternoon except Saturdays & Sundays.

Recruits required to
complete establishment:—

	Jan 4.	Feb. 9th
21st.	63	98
22nd.	78	119
23rd	29	~~64~~ 53
24th	73	~~27~~ 55
	233	~~370~~ 325

Note about 70 men have
been taken away from the
Brigade for Divisional Cyclist
Corp.

———

21st. 23rd, & 24th Bns.
report no drafts of recruits
from Reserve Battn.
22nd Battn reports one draft
of 29 — 18 of them returned
medically unfit.

———

To, Headquarters,

    1/6th London Infantry Brigade.

        With reference to your telephone message of today.

1. No. of recruits joined during January........10

2. No. of men discharged or transferred to
    Reserve Battn. during January.........14

3, No. required to complete....................53

John E. Thornhill Capt. & Adjt.,
for Comdg., 1/23rd Battn The London Regt.

ST ALBANS
9/2/15.

SKELETON FORM OF WAR DIARY.

Unit..........................

Brigade........................

Division.......................

Mobilization Centre............

Temporary War Station..........

Stations since occupied subsequent to concentration..............
....

(a) MOBILIZATION.

(b) CONCENTRATION AT WAR STATIONS (including Railway Moves)

(c) ORGANIZATION FOR DEFENCE (including vulnerable points)

(d) TRAINING.

(e) DISCIPLINE.

(f) ADMINISTRATION.

    1. Medical services.

    2. Veterinary services.

    3. Supply Services.

    4. Transport Services.

    5. Ordnance Services.

    6. Billetting and Hutting.

    7. Channels of correspondence in routine matters.

    8. Range construction.

    9. Supply of Remounts.

(g) REORGANIZATION OF T.F. INTO HOME AND IMPERIAL SERVICE.

(h) PREPARATION OF UNITS FOR IMPERIAL SERVICE.

===================================

Index............ ....

SUBJECT.

WAR DIARY

No.	Contents.	Date.
	General Staff 47th Div March 1915	

£ 6 6
2 8
2 16
4 0
3 10
£ 2 1

5 7
4
£ 20 8

Army Form C. 2118.

WAR DIARY
or
INTELLIGENCE SUMMARY.

General Staff.

47th Division. (1/2nd London)

MARCH 1915

Place	Date	Hour	Summary of Events and Information	Remarks and references to Appendices
ST.ALBANS	1st-5th March		G.O.C., G.S.O., A.A.& Q.M.G. and 130 other officers of the Division went to the Continent.	
"	4th	"	1/5th London Infantry Brigade being prepared first for service overseas Field firing at DUNSTABLE cancelled but ammunition expended on other Ranges.	
"	5th	"	All Courses of Instruction outside Divisional Billetting area cancelled.	
"	6th	"	Divisional Supply Column moved to BULFORD to be mobilized.	
"	"	"	1/5th London Infantry Brigade and Brigade Company Train (No.3) warned for embarkation Tuesday 9th inst.	
"	9th	"	Musketry being carried on.	
"	"	"	2/5th London Infantry Brigade No. 3 Coy. Train & Brigade Signal Section entrained at ST.ALBANS and HARPENDEN. The entrainment owing to previous practice worked smoothly and the units were ready loaded up to scheduled time. G.O.C. Third Army watched the loading of some trains at both places.	
" 9.45 a.m	15th	"	Divisional H.Q. left in one train for Port of Embarkation. Remainder of Division not already embarked, leaving 16th & 17th.	
	18th	"	Arrived destination for Divisional Area. Division H.Q. at MARLES-LES-MINES about 10 miles S. of LILLERS. The Division is in the I Corps, First Army.	
MARLES LES MINES	22nd March		Inspection of the Division by Field Marshal Sir John French.	

2nd LONDON DIVISION.

MARLES-LES-MINES.

23rd March 1915.

Dull morning. Some rain in evening.

Major B.F. Burnett-Hitchcock, D.S.O., Sherwood Foresters, took over G.S.O.2, from 4th Division.

Situation of Division :-

MARLES-LES-MINES.
Divl.H.Q., Cyclist Coy., Signal Coy., Mobile Vet.Secn., 4th Lon.Fd.Coy. R.E., Divl.Ammn.Col., and Heavy Battery.

FERFAY and AUCHEL.
4th Lon.Inf.Bde., 7th and 8th (Howr.) R.F.A. Brigades, M.T. Column, and 4th Lon.Fd. Ambce.

BURBURE and ALLOUAGNE.
5th Lon.Inf.Bde., 5th R.F.A. Bde., 5th Lon.Fd.Ambce.

NORRENT FONTES.
6th Lon.Inf.Bde., 6th Lon.R.F.A. Bde., 6th Lon.Fd.Ambce.

10.30 p.m.	Orders from 1st Corps for 6th, 7th and 8th Bns. of 4th Lon.Inf.Bde. to be prepared to move not before 2 p.m. 24th, for attachment to 2nd Division. -- -- -- -- -- --	G/448/1st Corps.
11.10 p.m.	Repeated to 4th Lon.Inf.Bde. -- -- --	G/18.

MARLES-LES-MINES.

24th March 1915.

Wet morning.

No change in situation.

Brig.Gen. R.A.K.Montgomery, Arty.Adv. 1st Corps, lectured Brigadiers, C.Os. and Adjts. on Artillery Co-operation in the Attack.

12 noon.	6th, 7th and 8th Bns. of 4th Lon.Inf.Bde. ordered to 2nd Divn. for trench training. Marched at 2 p.m. to BETHUNE. -- -- --	G/251/1st Corps.

Arrangements for attaching Brigadier of 4th Lon.Inf.Bde., and C.R.E., to 2nd Divn. commenced.

24th March (contd).

4.7 (H) Battery placed at disposal of
2nd Division temporarily. — — — —   138/G.1st Corps.
    Passed to Div.Arty.& returned.Secret.   No.29. B.M.C.7.

Instructions for distinguishing French
Airships and Signals. To be changed at
intervals. (Secret) — — — — —   250/G.1st Corps.
    Circulated Secret. — — —   No. 30.

G.S.O's 1 and 2, reconnoitred ridges
East of Division in case of being required
to occupy them to cover roads leading to West.

25th March 1915.

MARLES-LES-MINES.

Wet night and day until 5 p.m. Thick mist.

4th Lon.Fd.Co.R.E. moved to BEUVRY for
attachment to 2nd Division.

9-48 p.m.   1st Corps informs us 1st Divn. not
ready to take complete units for instruction
but can take officers and N.C.O's. Asks how   G/467.1st Corps.
many we wish to send. Asked 5th Lon.Inf.   G.T.27.
Bde. for numbers available. Replied 35   B.M.90.5th Bde.
Offrs.& 32 N.C.O's. Forwarded to 1st Corps.   G.28.

26th March 1915.

MARLES-LES-MINES.

Slight frost during night. Fine cold day.

G.S.O's 1 and 2, and G.O's C. 5th & 6th Lon.
Inf.Bdes. reconnoitred G.H.Q. 2nd & 3rd
Lines as allotted to 1st Corps.

Instructions received for one 5" How.
Batty. to be temporarily attached to Meerut   257/G.1st Corps.
Divn. from 3rd April. Asked 1st Corps   G/38.
re portions of Bde.& Div.A.C.accompanying.   G.T.29.

Instructions for rendering register of   252/G.1st Corps.
mines received. Secret.   G/39.

Morning air report gives indication of
considerable movement in area ROUBAIX –
ORCHIES – DOUAI – LENS by rail, general
tendency to be towards two last named places.   I.G/168.1st Corps

10-45 p.m.   15 Offrs.& 15 N.C.O's to be attached to
2nd & 3rd Inf.Bdes. from 28th instant (vide   G/476. 1st Corps
above). 5th Lon.Inf.Bde. warned.   G.34.

27th March 1915.

MARLES-LES-MINES.

Slight frost again. Bright day.
Attempt at snow.

6th Lon.Inf.Bde. etc and 6th F.A.Bde.
moved into billets about LAPUGNOY and
LABEUVRIERE. Situation attached as Appendix.

3.

27th March (contd).

9-30 a.m.	Telephone orders received from 1st Corps, afterwards confirmed by wire, for one How. Batty. to join MEERUT Div. on 30th, and Heavy Batty. to join No. 1 Group, Reserve Heavy Arty. on 28th. O.C's reporting personally for orders on those dates. How.Batty. at RIEZ BAILLEUL, Heavy at VIEILLE CHAPELLE. Orders issued to Divl.Arty.	G/480.1st C. G.36. B.M.71.D.Arty.
	Attachment of Officers and N.C.O's to 1st Divn. to be for 24 hours only. Parties relieving one another by bus. Attachment is to 2nd Inf.Bde. at OSE DU RAUX North of LOISNE and to 3rd Inf.Bde. at RICHEBOURG ST VAAST. 5th Lon.Inf.Bde.informed.	G/484.1st C. G.34, 42, & G.44.
	Reference instructions for training "Grenadiers". Applied for types of bombs and for dummies.	G.43
10-30 p.m.	Zeppelin seen 7 miles N.E. of CASSEL apparently heading for CALAIS. Lookout to be kept for it returning and 1st Corps to be informed. Circulated.	G/485.1st C. G.T.45.

Sunday, 28th March 1915.

MARLES-LES-MINES.

	Frost at night. Bright, cold, windy morning and throughout day.	
	Received from 1st Corps Plans of G.H.Q. 2nd & 3rd Lines. Secret. Filed by G.S.O. 3 with maps.	1st C. 107/G. G.46.
8-55 a.m.	Air report 6-20 - 7-30 a.m. No unusual movement in rear of German lines.	I.G/172.1st C.
6-0 p.m.	Asked if any restrictions to cutting wood for training purposes. Informed that this must not be done. Inf.Bdes. informed.	G.52. A.B./952. G.53.
7-8 p.m.	Air report 5-20 - 6-10 p.m. One cavalry regt. moving towards HERLIES from AUBERS.	I.G/177.1st C.
	G.S.O.2 attended conference of 6th Lon. Inf.Bde. Arranged with Q for wire for training.	

29th March 1915.

MARLES-LES-MINES.

	Hard frost at night. Bright, cold, windy day.	
10-0 a.m.	G.O.C. inspected Divl.Ammn.Col.	
	Orders re issue of encouraging and congratulatory orders.	168/G.1st C.
	Officers, N.C.O's & Telephonists of R.A. attached to 1st & 2nd Divns. for 3 clear days, commences today.	

4.

29th March (contd).

1 Offr.& 2 Gunners R.A., and 1 Offr. & 2 Privates Infantry, to report at MAISON ANDRIEN, Rue du Nord, ST.VENANT tomorrow, for Trench Mortar course.	2118/2.1st Corps. G.48.

4-30 p.m.   Orders for attachment of R.A.Officers to 2nd Divn. and for move of batteries to that Divnl.area to come under command of 2nd Divn.
      Move of Officers on 30th March.   265/G. 1st Corps.
      ,,   5" (How) Batty. on 2nd April.   G.50.
      ,,   15 pdr Bdes. on 3rd April.   G.60.
Lon.Div.Arty. & A & Q informed.   1st Corps asked re S.A.A.Secns of Bde. & Divl.Ammn.Cols.

30th March 1915.

MARLES-LES-MINES.
      Hard frost and very cold night.

7-50 a.m.   Div.Engrs.to arrange supply of stakes and brushwood for training purposes.   G.62.

      G.S.O's 1 and 2 visited CUINCHY trenches.

10-19 a.m.   Air report. No movement.

3-55 p.m.   Orders for move of Howr.Batty to Indian Divn. cancelled.   Div.Arty.informed.   G/503. 1st Corps. I.G.64.

4-15 p.m.   Orders for moves of remainder of Arty. (except Heavy Batty) cancelled. Div.Arty.infd.   G/502. 1st Corps. I.G.65.

5-15 p.m.   Orders issued for officers to visit bomb factory, 78 Rue de Lille, BETHUNE, at 3 p.m. on 1st April.   G.67.

      Orders for reports to reach Corps H.Q. 7 p.m. Forwarded to Inf.Bdes. for reports to reach Div.H.Q. at 6 p.m. when Divn. is in the line.   266/G. 1st Corps. G/51.

31st March 1915.

MARLES-LES-MINES.
      Slight frost during night. Less wind. Warmer day.
      G.S.O's 1 & 2 visited GIVENCHY trenches (4th Guards Brigade).

9-35 a.m.   Air report. No movements behind German lines.   I.G/183. 1st C.
      Instructions for sketches, tracings, etc to be based on 1/5,000 maps.   271/G. 1st Corps. G/53.

5-20 p.m.   German air reconnaissance generally takes place at 3 a.m. at present.   G/521. 1st Corps.

7-55 p.m.   3 Battns with 2nd Divn.leave there on morning of 7th April to rejoin. Probably replaced by 3 others.   G/483. 2nd Divn.
Asked 2nd Div. for attachment of Brigadiers of 5th and 6th Lon.Inf.Bdes.   G.75.

31st March (contd).

11-0 p.m.	1st Corps asks battalions to go to 1st Divn. on 2nd April. Two battns, and may have to move on 1st. 15th & 17th Battns of 4th & 5th Lon.Inf.Bdes. warned (subsequently cancelled) and 1st Corps informed, (also cancelled). Cancellation due to it being more suitable to detail battns of 6th Lon. Inf.Bde. who save a day's marching owing to their present position in billets.	G/515. 1st Corps. I.G.77 & 78. B.M.127. 5th Bde. S.C.123. 4th Bde.

WAR DIARY (contd).

Hour, date, place.	Summary of events & information.	Remarks & references to Appendices.
ST ALBANS		
2/3/1915	Company training. 3rd class shots musketry.	
3/3/1915	Kit inspection Medical inspection.	
4/3/1915	Company training. 3rd class shots musketry.	

ST ALBANS
9/3/15.

[signature] 2/Lt. a/Adjt.

[signature] fr. Lieut. Colonel,
Commanding, 1/23rd Battalion The London Regiment.

COMPOSITION OF 1/2nd LONDON DIVISION

BOOKLET DATED 1st MARCH 1915.

S.D.2

Distribution	
GS	1
AA&QMG	1
Signals	1
Ordnance Officer	1
ADMS	1
3 Inf Bdes	3
CRA	1
CRE	1
4 F.A. Bde	4
ASC	1

No spare copy for file.

COPY TELEGRAM.

Received 12.55 p.m.
2nd March 1915.

Second London Division
    St.Albans

Q 934 March 2nd AAA The 2nd London Division is to be completed at once for service on the continent AAA Instructions regarding completing of equipment and clothing and for formation of certain line of communication units will be issued separately AAA Division proceeds without any Divisional cavalry AAA 2/3rd London Field Company and 1/4th London Field Co will accompany Division AAA Submit earliest possible date return showing strength of various units of division conditions for service as laid down in para 4 of War Office letter No 9/London/147 dated 28th October 1914 that is medically fit for service fully trained and 19 years of age or over Acknowledge receipt addressed 2nd London Division repeated Third Army

                CENTRAFORCE   LONDON

Telephone
 1/4th Inf. Bde
1/5 & 1/6

All Officers and N.C.O's now attending Courses of Instruction outside Divisional Billeting area are being recalled.

All arrangements for attendance of Officers and N.C.O's at future Courses are cancelled.

12.30 p.m.
3. March 1915

"C" Form (Duplicate). Army Form C. 2123
MESSAGES AND SIGNALS. No. of Message

| | Charges to Pay. £ s. d. | Office Stamp. |

OB
3rd mch

Service Instructions.

OHMS

Handed in at Gt. Dunmow Office 2 37 p.m. Received 2 41 p.m.

TO Hdqrs 2nd Lon Divn
St Albans

| Sender's Number | Day of Month | In reply to Number | AAA |
| ga 527 | mch 3 | | |

Reference your 9/185 dated march 2nd centrafore of return of field coy from brightlingsea tomorrow AAA Train arrangement will be forwarded to O. C. concerned

FROM Third army
PLACE & TIME

Urgent *Office copy*

COPY TELEGRAM.

Received 2.48 p.m.
3rd March 1915.

Headquarters,
    2nd London Division,   St.Albans.

Ga 527 March 3 Reference your G/185 dated March 2nd Centraforce sanctions return of Field Company from Brightlingsea tomorrow AAA Train arrangement will be forwarded to O.C. concerned

        Thirdarmy.

C.R.E.,
    1/2nd London Division.

        Forwarded.

E.H. Collen
Major,
General Staff,
1/2nd London Division T.F.

[GENERAL STAFF 2ND LONDON DIVISION
No. G/338.
3 MAR. 915
TERRITORIAL FORCE]

[Copy to Q. Branch
3/3/15]

URGENT.

FILE COPY.

K.E.H.
C.R.E.
1/4th Lon.Inf.Bde.
1/5th   do
1/6th   do

Reference this office G/309/8 dated 27/2/15, all Officers and N.C.O's attending Course in Explosives at SHEFFIELD have been ordered to rejoin their units tomorrow early.

E.H. Cotten
Major,
General Staff,
1/2nd London Division T.F.

URGENT.

FILE COPY

Headquarters,
1/6th London Infantry Brigade.

Reference this office G/185/5 dated 23/2/15, all N.C.O's attending Course in Cookery at Hyde Park Barracks have been ordered to rejoin their units tomorrow early.

E.H. Collen
Major,
General Staff,
1/2nd London Division T.F.

Courses of Instruction

	now attending	Warned
Lon. District at Chelsea.	6 Offrs.) 5th Inf. Bde. 6 N.C.Os.) Ref. 82/10	3 Offrs.) 6th Inf. Bde. 4 N.C.Os.) Ref. 82/11
Field Telephones at Aldershot	nil Ref. 114.	nil
Musketry at Bisley	5 Offrs.) 3 Inf. Bdes 5 N.C.Os.) Ref. 129/12 1 Offr.) 4th Inf. Bde. 4 N.C.Os.) do. 5th Inf. Bde. Ref. 129/13	
Co-Operation betn. Arty. & Aircraft at Salisbury Plain	2 Offrs. R.A. Ref. 161/11	
Cookery at Aldershot	1 N.C.O. 6th Inf. Bde. Ref. 185/1	1 N.C.O. 5th Bde. Ref. 185/2
Cookery at Hyde Park Barracks	2 N.C.Os 6th Inf. Bde. 185/5	

Cable Laying   nil   nil
   at Aldershot
                     Ref. 243.

Explosives &c.
   at Shenfield   7 Offrs. } K.E.H.
                3 NCOs } C.R.E.
                         & 3 Bdrs.
                Ref. 309/6

Ordnance College
   Woolwich   5 Offrs. R.A.
                Ref. 318.

Pontoon Training
   at Egham.   Ref. 5/79
                File to Q. Branch.

"A" Form.   Army Form C. 2121.

MESSAGES AND SIGNALS.

TO: 2nd Lon Div

Sender's Number	Day of Month	In reply to Number	
G.541	3rd		AAA

The 6th 7th and 8th City of Lon Battns will be assembled in Their billets in BETHUNE on the evening of 6th April and on 7th April they will march as under from BETHUNE to the billets formerly occupied by then in 2nd Lon Div Area aaa 6th Bn to RAIMBERT via PONT DU REVEILLON LOZINGHEM and AUCHEL Head to pass Level crossing E4A at 8 am aaa 7th Bn and 8th Bn to AUCHEL via PONT DU REVEILLON and LOZINGHEM Head to pass level crossing

(Z)

Wt. W1154/2240. 7/11. 7,500,000. Sch. 4a. "A" Form. Army Form C. 2121.

MESSAGES AND SIGNALS.

ELA	at	8.30 am	and	9 am
respectively aaa		Billeting	parties	and
Cooks	will	be	sent	ahead
under	Battn	arrangements	but	must
clear	level	crossing	ELA	by
7.55	am	aaa	Infy	Bde
Commanders	2nd	Div	will	see
that	these	orders	are	communicated
to	the	Bn	attached to them	
Bdes	aaa	Addressed	4th	5th
and	6th	Bdes	Repld	2nd
Lon	Div	and	Town Commandant
BETHUNE				

From Second Div.
Place
Time 7-10 pm

4/8/05

Wt. W1154/2240. 7/11. 7,500,000. Sch. 4a.	"A" Form.			Army Form C. 2121.
	MESSAGES AND SIGNALS.			No. of Message ____

Prefix ____ Code ____ m.	Words	Charge	This message is on a/c of:	Recd. at ____ m.
Office of Origin and Service Instructions.				Date ____
	Sent		____ Service.	From ____
	At ____ m.			
	To ____			By ____
	By		(Signature of "Franking Officer.")	

TO	42	bgn	Inf	Bde

Sender's Number.	Day of Month	In reply to Number		AAA
G.T. 115	3rd			

6th	7th	8th	Bns	march
from	BETHUNE	7th	April	via
PONT	DU	REVEILLON		LOZINGHEM
and	AUCHEL	aaa	Heads	of
Columns	in	order	of	Battns
named	pass	E.4.A.	Level	Crossing
at	8 am	8-30 am	and	9 am
respectively.	aaa	Billeting	parties	
and	Cooks	clear	E.4.B	day
7.55	am			

From				
Place				
Time				

The above may be forwarded as now corrected. (Z)

Censor. Signature of Addressor or person authorised to telegraph in his name.

* This line should be erased if not required.

COPY OF TELEGRAM.

"2nd.London Division, St.Albans.

Q.977 March 5th AAA The 2/3rd.London Field Company R.E., will not accompany the 2nd.London Division overseas AAA This Division will proceed abroad with the 1/4th.London Field Company R.E., only AAA Preparation of 2/3rd.London Field Company R.E., is not to be proceeded with AAA Acknowledge receipt AAA Addressed 2nd.London Division repeated Third Army.

Centraforce London."

General Staff.

The above copy of telegram is forwarded for your information.

Q 158/3

Lt.Colonel,
St.Albans.   A.A.&.Q.M.G., 1/2nd.London Division.

SECRETARY
   WAR OFFICE
      LONDON

G 199 FEBRUARY 7 IT HAS BEEN ASCERTAINED FROM
O.C. 1/3rd LONDON BRIGADE ARTILLERY THAT NO
EXTENSIONS TO GUN SHIELDS OR SHIELDS TO WAGONS
HAVE YET BEEN FIXED AAA DESIRABLE THAT 1/7th
LONDON BRIGADE ARTILLERY EQUIPMENT SHOULD
BE HANDED OVER TO 1/3rd BRIGADE AAA
ORDERS HAVE BEEN ISSUED TO THOROUGHLY
DISINFECT 1/7th EQUIPMENT AAA KINDLY
WIRE INSTRUCTIONS AAA

ONE SECOND LONDON DIVISION
ST ALBANS

W. General Wray telephones:—

" The 1/3rd Bde R.F.A. telegraph:—
There are no extensions to gun shields
No shields on waggons.
No vehicles have been altered in any way "

———

The obvious solution is to exchange the
guns & waggons of 1/3rd Bde for those
of 1/7th Bde.

Will General Wolfe kindly take this
up with Colonel Bingham or someone
else at War Office.

General Wray wanted to send an
Officer to the War Office, but I told
he had better not do so.

P.W.
7.3.13

CENTRAFORCE
        HORSE GUARDS
              LONDON

G 199   FEB 7

THE FOLLOWING WIRE HAS THIS DAY BEEN SENT TO WAR OFFICE BEGINS IT HAS BEEN ASCERTAINED FROM O.C.1/3rd LONDON BRIGADE ARTILLERY THAT NO EXTENSIONS TO GUN SHIELDS OR SHIELDS TO WAGONS HAVE YET BEEN FIXED AAA DESIRABLE THAT 1/7th LONDON BRIGADE ARTILLERY EQUIPMENT SHOULD BE HANDED OVER TO 1/3rd BRIGADE AAA ORDERS HAVE BEEN ISSUED TO THOROUGHLY DISINFECT 1/7th EQUIPMENT AAA KINDLY WIRE INSTRUCTIONS AAA MESSAGE ENDS

ONE SECOND LONDON DIVISION
       ST ALBANS

> Any further communication on this subject should be addressed to—
>
> The Secretary,
> War Office,
> London, S.W.,
>
> and the following number quoted.

120/General Number/7735 (Q.M.G.2.)

**War Office,
London, S.W.**

8th March, 1915.

Sir,

I am directed to forward the following Instructions for distribution in the Division under your Command in accordance with the attached list, and to request that you will be good enough to acknowledge receipt of the same in due course :-

Instructions for Entrainment and
Embarkation of Units of the
Expeditionary Force, Part I .... 145 copies

   - do -   Part II .... 145 ,,

Standing Orders for the
Expeditionary Force .... 148 ,,

Owing to shortness of time the necessary Instructions for the 1/5th London Brigade have been despatched direct.

I am,

Sir,

Your obedient servant.

R Stuart Wortley

Director of Movements.

The General Officer Commanding,
   1/2nd London Division,
      St Albans.

1/2nd LONDON DIVISION.

Distribution of Instructions.

Unit etc.	Instructions for Entrainment & Embarkation, Part I.	Instructions for Entrainment & Embarkation, Part II.	Standing Orders for the E.F.
Divisional Head Qrs.	3	3	6
Head Qrs. 1/4th London Bde.	2	2	2
1/6th Bn. London Regt.	4	4	10
1/7th Bn. London Regt.	4	4	10
1/8th Bn. London Regt.	4	4	10
1/15th Bn. London Regt.	4	4	10
Head Qrs. 1/6th London Bde.	2	2	2
1/21st Bn. London Regt.	4	4	10
1/22nd Bn. London Regt.	4	4	10
1/23rd Bn. London Regt.	4	4	10
1/24th Bn. London Regt.	4	4	10
1/2nd London Div. Cyclist Coy.	2	2	2
Head Qrs. Divisional Artillery	2	2	2
1/5th London Bde. R.F.A.	11	11	6
1/6th London Bde. R.F.A.	11	11	6
1/3rd London Bde. R.F.A.	11	11	6
1/8th London (How:) Bde R.F.A.	10	10	6
1/2nd London Heavy Batt: & Ammunition Col:	4	4	4
1/2nd London Div: Amm: Col:	15	15	6
Head Qrs. Divisional Engineers	2	2	2
1/4th London Field Co. R.E.	3	3	2
1/2nd London Div. Signal Co.	9	9	5
1/2nd London Divisional Train	14	14	5
1/4th London Field Ambulance	4	4	2
1/5th ,, ,,	4	4	2
1/6th ,, ,,	4	4	2
	145	145	148

Herewith copies of the undermentioned books, for distribution to units as shown on the attached sheet :-

Instructions for Entrainment and
    Embarkation of units of the
    Expeditionary Force, Part I.   *   *   Copies.

    - do -   *   Part II,   *   *   ,,

Standing Orders for the
    Expeditionary Force.   *   *   *   ,,

Kindly acknowledge receipt hereon.

[signature]
Lt.Colonel,
General Staff,
1/2nd London Division T.F.

G/345
St.Albans.
9th March 1918.

1/2nd LONDON DIVISION, T.F.

DISTRIBUTION OF INSTRUCTIONS.

Unit etc.	Instructions for Entrainment and Embarkation, Part I.	Instructions for Entrainment and Embarkation, Part II.	Standing Orders for the Ex.F.
Divisional Hd.Qrs.	3	3	6
Hd.Qrs.1/4th L.Inf.Bde.	2	2	2
1/6th Bn.Lon.Reg.	4	4	10
1/7th ,,	4	4	10
1/8th ,,	4	4	10
1/15th ,,	4	4	10
Hd.Qrs.1/6th L.Inf.Bde.	2	2	2
1/21st Bn.Lon.Regt.	4	4	10
1/22nd ,,	4	4	10
1/23rd ,,	4	4	10
1/24th ,,	4	4	10
1/2nd Lon.Div.Cyclist Co.	2	2	2
Hd.Qrs.Div.R.A.	2	2	2
1/5th Lon.Bde.R.F.A.	11	11	6
1/6th ,,	11	11	6
1/3rd ,,	11	11	6
1/8th (How)	10	10	6
1/2nd Lon.Heavy Batt & Amn. Column.	4	4	4
1/2nd Lon.Divl.A.Col.	15	15	6
Hd.Qrs. Divl. R.E.	2	2	2
1/4th Lon.Fd.Co.R.E.	3	3	2
1/2nd Lon.Div.Sig.Co.	9	9	5
1/2nd Lon.Div.Train.	14	14	5
1/4th Lon.Fd.Ambulance.	4	4	2
1/5th ,,	4	4	2
1/6th ,,	4	4	2

St.Albans.
9th March 1915.
G/343

From Brig. Gen J. C. Wray, M.V.O.
    Commanding Divisional Artillery,
        1/2nd London Division, T.F.

To   G. O. C.,
        1/2nd London Division.

Sir,

I have the honour to report that I visited the 1/3rd London F. A. Brigade in Rickmansworth Park to-day.

(1) The horses appeared to be well on the whole, but dirty. There were, however, several cases of mange in the Brigade Ammunition Column, and about 190 horses will be required to replace casualties, etc.

(2) There are 107 men to be replaced (Medically Unfit, Home Service, etc.), but none of the men belonging to the Reserve Brigade have received any training in Gunnery.

The Brigade is 3 Officers short, in addition tot the 6 extra Subalterns which have been sanctioned for training, and I am informed by the Staff Officer, R.A. who has seen the Reserve Brigade in London, that they are much below the low standard of efficiency of the Reserve Units.

(3) The equipment was not in good order. There was a good deal of play in the Rocking Bar Sights which should have been taken up by the Brigade's own Artificers - this will take a considerable time to rectify. No tops have been provided for the gun shields. These will take at least 3 weeks to make and fit. nor have the wagons any shields fitted.

(4) The Brigade has no telephones, and have not purchased any private ones as was done by the Batteries of the 1/2nd Lon. Divl. Arty. some 3 months ago. They will therefore be very much behind the rest of the Divisional Artillery in this all important point.

(5). Very few of the Officers Field Glasses have been graticuled which must prove a severe handicap in enabling effective fire to be brought to bear.

(6). No musketry practice has been carried out.

(7). The last part of the Brigade was only marching in as I was leaving at about 1-30 p.m. and from the way the vehicles etc were moving along the road, I should say that the march discipline of the Brigade was inferior.

(8). On the whole I was not favourably impressed with the appearance of the Brigade. I am inclined to think that the Division would have been better off with the personnel of the 1/7th London F.A. Brigade as they have

taken part in the progressive training of the Division and the capabilities of all the Officers, from an Artillery point of view, are well known to me.

(9) I am of opinion that it would have been better to have exchanged horses and men of the 1/7th London F.A. Brigade and to have destroyed the Grooming Kit, and has the mens clothes disinfected.

       I have the honour to be,

        Sir,

       Your obedient Servant,

        (sd) C. Wray, Br. Genl.

No. 3093   Comdg. Divl. Arty.
9th March 1915.   1/2nd London Division T.F.

S/346

From,

    Major General C.St.L. Barter, G.V.O., C.B.,

        Commanding 1/2nd London Division, T.F.,

To,

    The General Officer Commanding

        3rd Army, Central Force.

∞∞∞∞∞∞∞∞∞∞∞∞∞∞∞∞∞∞∞∞∞∞∞∞∞∞∞∞∞∞∞∞∞∞∞∞

                                St.Albans,

                                10th March 1915.

Sir,

        With reference to the posting of the 1/3rd London Field Artillery Brigade to this Division in place of the 1/7th London Brigade R.F.A., I have the honour to forward a report from my C.R.A. on a preliminary inspection which he made yesterday of the new Brigade.

        I myself inspected the 1/3rd London Field Artillery Brigade this morning.

        I found that the batteries manoeuvred creditably. The men are well set up and ride well, and the horses are in good condition, though in the majority of cases extremely dirty. The brigade is, however, very backward in some respects and cannot be compared with the 1/7th F.A.Brigade in readiness for service. Amongst the most important unfavourable points which I noted were the following :-

(a). The bad state of the equipment, as pointed out in paragraph 3 of the attached report by my C.R.A.

(b). The deficiency in telephones and in telephone instruction.

(c). Shortage of 107 men for which no trained men are forthcoming from the reserve units of the brigade.

(d). The unserviceable state of a large proportion of the harness of the batteries, for the renewal of which no indents have yet been put in.

(e). Great deficiency in equipment generally and bad state of clothing.

                                                (f)

(f). No gun practice since 1913, and no musketry practice at all.

(g). The mangy condition of many of the horses of the small arms section of the Ammunition Column, which has necessitated the isolation of the horses of the Section.

(h). The dirty turn-out generally of the units, especially as regards the horses.

For these reasons I venture again most earnestly to express the hope that the 1/7th London Field Artillery Brigade may be retained with the Division.

Should, however, this measure not be sanctioned, I would recommend that the guns and wagons of the two brigades should be exchanged and that a sufficiency of Officers and trained men be transferred to complete the 1/3rd London F.A. Brigade up to establishment. I consider these measures indispensable.

I have the honour to be,

Sir,

Your obedient Servant,

C. Barter

Major General,
Commanding 1/2nd London Division,
T.F.

COPY

The Secretary
    War Office
        London, S.W.
================================

Herewith Army Form A.24 for 1915.

The Secret Books and Documents enumerated thereon have been handed over to the G.O.C. 2/2nd London Division T.F., and a receipt has been obtained.

St. Albans.

[signature]
for
Major General,
Commanding 1/2nd London Division T.F.

[Stamp: GENERAL STAFF 2ND LONDON DIVISION — TERRITORIAL FORCE — No. — 14 MAR 1915]

CONFIDENTIAL Copy

G/2

Headquarters

   1st Army Corps.

In accordance with instructions given verbally to Lt.Colonel Thwaites today, I forward the following proposals for the employment of battalions in the Division under my command in the trenches for a 72 hours instructional period when required:-

(a). When 4 Brigades are occupying the trenches.

Period.	Unit.	Brigade of Allotment.
1st Period of 72 hours.	24th London Regiment.	5th Brigade.
	23rd ,,	4th ,,
	20th ,,	1st ,,
	15th ,,	2nd ,,
2nd Period of 72 hours.	22nd London Regiment.	5th Brigade.
	19th ,,	4th ,,
	18th ,,	1st ,,
	8th ,,	2nd ,,
3rd Period of 72 hours.	21st London Regiment.	5th Brigade.
	17th ,,	4th ,,
	7th ,,	1st ,,
	6th ,,	2nd ,,

(b). When 6 Brigades are occupying the trenches.

Period.	Unit.	Brigade of Allotment.
1st Period of 72 hours.	24th London Regiment.	6th Brigade.
	23rd ,,	5th ,,
	20th ,,	4th ,,
	19th ,,	1st ,,
	15th ,,	2nd ,,
	8th ,,	3rd ,,
2nd Period of 72 hours.	22nd London Regiment.	6th Brigade.
	21st ,,	5th ,,
	18th ,,	4th ,,
	17th ,,	1st ,,
	7th ,,	2nd ,,
	6th ,,	3rd ,,

If this arrangement is approved, I will notify G.O's C. Infantry Brigades under my command to hold these units in readiness when the time comes.

                                            Major General,

                        Commanding 2nd London Division
                                                T.F.

1st CORPS.

Return of feeding strength for week ending 20th March 1915.

UNIT	Officers	Other Ranks		
1st DIVISION				
1st Bn. Coldstream Gds.	19	935		1
1st Bn. Scots Guards	14	869	1	2
1st Bn. R. Highdrs.	26	961		
1st Cameron Hdrs	25	1007		
London Scottish	29	889		
2nd Royal Sussex R.	33	944	3	272
1st L.North Lancs Regt.	23	801		
1st Northamptonsh. R.	19	977		
2nd K.R.Rifle Corps	24	1071		
8th R. Sussex Regt	52	902		
1st S.Wales Bordrs	20	1009	2	
1st Bn. Gloucester	26	986	1	
2nd The Welsh Regt	23	969	2	
2nd R. Mun. Fusiliers	28	848	1	
4th R. Welsh Fus.	26	528	1	112
9th K.L'pool Regt	28	938		
	395	14289	11	387
2nd DIVISION.				
2nd Grenadier Gds	18	1069		
2nd Coldstream Gds.	19	987		
3rd Coldstream Gds.	19	973		
1st Irish Gds	27	1094		
1st Herts Regt	21	840		
2nd R. Innis. Fusiliers	26	977		
2nd Worcester Regt	22	1015		
2nd Ox. & Bucks L.I.	29	984	3	
2nd Highland L.I.	26	1042	5	
9th " "	26	988		
1st King's L'pool R.	24	1034		
2nd E.Staff. Regt.	26	1036		
1st R. Berks. Regt	22	970		
1st Kings. R.R.Corps	26	963		
1/5th King's L'pool R.	26	1080		
1/7th " "	31	1009		
	395	16907	8	
2nd LONDON DIVISION.				
5th Bn. London Regt.	29	996		
7th " " "	30	996		
8th " " "	30	991		
15th " " "	30	963		
17th " " "	28	987		
18th " " "	27	993		
19th " " "	30	976		
20th " " "	30	990		
21st " " "	29	921		
22nd " " "	28	988		
23rd " " "	28	985		
24th " " "	30	990		
	348	11489		
1st Bn. The Queen's Regt.	28	816		
TOTAL	1164	42868	19	387
			19	387
			1183	43255

H.Q. 1st Corps.
21/3/15.

SECRET.

2 Lon Div/259/G

Copy No. 3

1st CORPS OPERATION ORDER No. 75.

21st March 1915.

1. The 1st Corps will take over the front defensive line now held by the Indian Corps and the right of the 4th Corps up to but not including the road running N.W. from LA RUSSIE through M.35 c, b, and a. to M.34 b. This relief as regards infantry will be completed by 6 a.m. 25th March.

2. The 2nd Division will take over on the night March 22nd/23rd the front now held by 1st Division up to and including the road running N.E. from RUE du CAILLOUX through S.20 c. and d. and S.21 c.

3. The 1st Division will send tomorrow (22nd March) to the 8th Division area one battalion to take over that portion of the front now held by the 4th Corps about to be transferred to 1st Corps. This battalion will be attached to the 8th Division until the 1st Division relieves the left section of the Indian Corps, when it will again come under the 1st Division (see paragraph 4).

4. The 1st Division will take over the front now held by the Division of the Indian Corps on the nights 23rd/24th and 24th/25th March.

5. All details affecting the reliefs in paragraphs 2, 3 and 4 will be arranged between the Divisions concerned. Both Divisions will report progress of reliefs daily.

6. Artillery reliefs between the 1st and 2nd Divisions, and between the 1st Division and the Indian Divisions will be arranged direct between Divisions and will be completed by 6 a.m. 27th March.

7. The areas allotted to 1st and 2nd Divisions respectively are as shown in maps issued herewith. They will come into force from 6 a.m. 25th March.

R.Whigham
Brigadier-General,
General Staff, 1st Corps.

Issued at 5 p.m.
to:-
    1st Division.
    2nd Division.
    2nd London Division.
    Indian Corps.
    4th Corps.
    1st Bn Queens Regt.

Copy

Headquarters

1st Army Corps.

With reference to my letter No. G/2, dated 19th March 1915, the following is the order in which I would recommend battalions under my command being employed in the trenches for an instructional period of 72 hours :-

6th Battalion, London Regiment.
7th   ,,   ,,
8th   ,,   ,,
15th   ,,   ,,
17th   ,,   ,,
18th   ,,   ,,
19th   ,,   ,,
20th   ,,   ,,
21st   ,,   ,,
22nd   ,,   ,,
23rd   ,,   ,,
24th   ,,   ,,

C. Barter

Major General,
Commanding 2nd London Division T.F.

THIS FILE IS NOT TO BE FOLDED.

CENTRAL REGISTRY.

Central Registry No. and Date.	7185	Reference Files.
7185. 13436 23. 3. 15.	SUBJECT.	

Report on Disembarkation &c
2nd London Division

Referred to	Date	Referred to	Date	Referred to	Date
				Filed	Date.

SCHEDULE OF CORRESPONDENCE.

Sub. No.	Date	To Whom	Précis

Sub. No.	Date	To Whom	Précis

NOT TO BE WRITTEN ON.

A.A.G. to see

1) Please take up the question brought to notice in Capt. Turner's report with the Embarkation Comdt, Southampton.

2) Obtain Major White's report on the transport of the Division if he has made one

3) Then forward the whole lot to DJAG — & state that we have dealt with the question referred to in para 1. above.

H.T. Williams
D.J.
Base Comdt Havre

23/3/15

Headquarters,

    I. G. C.

    Herewith reports on the Disembarkation, Entraining and Transport of the 1/2nd. London Division.

    The question of Officers of Headquarter Units accompanying headquarter personnel on the same ship has been taken up with the Embarkation Commandant, Southampton.

Le Havre.
26/3/15.

                    Brigadier-General,
                    Base Commandant.

REPORT ON THE DISEMBARKATION OF THE 2nd LONDON
TERRITORIAL DIVISION.

The number of days of actual disembarking were seven.

An Infantry Brigade was sent over in advance arriving here on the 10th and 11th March. The remainder of the Division started to arrive on the 15th March and continued till the 18th March when there was an interval of two days, and on the 21st the Divisional Ammunition Column arrived so that the actual time that it took to complete the Division over here was eleven days.

I understand that the Divisional Ammunition Column was detained in England to be equipped with fresh horses as the original ones had contracted mange.

All units were sent up to the Rest Camp on arrival with the exception of the Divisional Ammunition Column and owing to high water being at an early hour in the morning the Artillery and Regimental Transport of practically all units were able to get up to Camp before dark.

The small "butterfly" boats were all berthed at the Quai d'Escale, and on one day as many as nine of these boats were berthed there at once. The whole of these were cleared and sailed in about two hours after the disembarkation commenced.

I consider that the practice of sending the bulk of the troops over on these ships most satisfactory. They are disembarked at 7.0 a.m. each morning and the troops are up in Camp early in the day.

With regard to the Divisional Ammunition Column their horses were issued to them at the last minute no harness having been fitted at all. In spite of this and

-2-

being rather short of time they were at their entraining point at the time ordered which I think was a very good performance and reflects credit on the unit.

The usual temporary A.M.L.O.s were sent over and they all were keen on their work and were very useful especially Captain J.W.Pace, 24th London Regiment whose services were a great benefit.

I attach a list of the ships that arrived with time table, etc. All the ships were berthed at the Quays as requested, and in very good time.

Havre.   Major.
22/3/15.   M.L.O.

RECORD OF TRANSPORT FOR 2nd LONDON DIVISION.

Name of ship.	Hour due.	Hour reported in the Roads.	Hour entering Port.	Hour berthed.	Hour discharged.	Name of Quay.	Remarks.
March 10th:-							
Viper.	4.50 a.m.		4.10 a.m.	4.35 a.m.	8.45 a.m.	Escale.	
Copenhagen.	4.15 "		3.45 "	4.15 "	8.0 "	"	
Queen Alexandra.	5.0 "		3.50 "	4.50 "	8.50 "	"	
Trafford Hall.	3.0 "		5.20 "	6.5 "	12.15 noon	Plata O	
Rossetti.	3.0 "		4.5 "	4.30 "	12.30 "	Pondicherry	
Duchess of Argyll.	4.0 "		3.20 "	4.0 "	7.40 a.m.	Escale.	
March 11th:-							
Munich.	1.30 a.m.		1.50 a.m.	2.30 a.m.	7.45 a.m.	Escale.	
Empress Queen.	1.30 "		2.0 "	2.30 "	7.45 "	"	
Courtfield.	3.0 "		3.50 "	4.15 "	11.40 "	Pondichery.	
March 15th:-							
Copenhagen.	3.30 a.m.		5.50 a.m.	6.20 a.m.	8.15 a.m.	Escale.	
Viper.	3.30 "		3.50 "	4.0 "	8.15 "	"	
Mount Temple.	5.0 "	6.30 a.m.	8.30 "	10.0 "	4.5 p.m.	Pondichery.	
Trafford Hall.	5.30 "	6.30 "	8.30 "	10.0 "	5.0 "	Plata O.	
City of Dunkirk.	5.30 "	6.30 "	8.30 "	10.0 "	4.50 "	Pondichery.	
March 16th:-							
Empress Queen.	1.30 a.m.	3.0 a.m.	5.40 a.m.	4.0 a.m.	8.15 a.m	Escale.	
Munich.	1.30 "	5.0 "	3.40 "	4.0 "	8.30 "	"	
Anglo Canadian.	5.50 "	5.50 "	9.15 "	10.0 "	5.0 p.m	Pondicherry.	
Clgebasna.	4.0 "	4.0 "	9.15 "	10.15 "	5.50 "	"	
Kathiranm.	4.0 "	5.30 "	9.0 "	10.0 "	4.30 "	Plata O.	

Name of ship.	Hour due.	Hour reported in the Roads.	Hour entering Port.	Hour berthed.	Hour discharged.	Name of Quay.	Remarks.
March 17th:-							
Queen Alexandra.	1.0 a.m.		1.0 a.m.	1.30 a.m.	7.45 a.m.	Escale.	
Inventor.	4.30 "	6.30 a.m.	9.50 "	10.20 "	4.15 p.m.	Pondichery.	
Architect.	4.30 "	8.0 "	9.30 "	10.15 "	5.10 "	"	
March 18th:-							
Marguerite.	2.0 a.m.		5.20 a.m.	4.0 a.m.	8.30 a.m.	Escale.	
Duchess of Montrse	3.0 "		4.30 "	4.30 "	8.0 "	"	
Empress Queen.	2.50 "		4.0 "	4.30 "	8.15 "	"	
Jupiter.			4.30 "	5.0 "	9.30 "	"	
Belmoral.			4.55 "	5.30 "	8.50 "	"	
Atlanta.			5.0 "	5.35 "	8.0 "	"	
Blackwell.	4.0 "	8.30 a.m	10.45 "	11.15 "	6.0 p.m	Plata O.	
Courtfield.	4.0 "	8.30 "	10.35 "	11.50 "	5.10 "	Pondichery.	
City of Chester	3.30 "	8.30 "	11.0 "	noon	4.30 "	Pondichery.	
March 21st:-							
Empress Queen.	1.30 a.m.		1.30 a.m.	2.0 a.m.	8.10 a.m	Escale.	
Caledonian.	5.0 "	6.50 a.m.	11.20 "	12.30 p.m.	4.45 p.m.	Pondichery.	
Archimedes.	5.0 "	6.30 "	10.30 "	11.40 a.m.	5.0 "	"	

Report on the Disembarkation and Entrainment of the
1/2nd. London (Territorial)Division.

The disembarkation and entrainment of this Division
worked smoothly and well. The temporary Assistant Military
Landing Officers and Entraining Officers sent over ahead of
the Division performed their duties in an intelligent
and energetic manner.
The Officer Commanding 1/2nd. London Divisional
Ammunition Column informed me that 100 of his horses and th
their harness (unfitted) had only been handed over to
him on the day previous to sailing. The fact that they
were able to entrain within 12 hours of the ship entering
port reflects great credit on the unit.
It has been observed in the case of Headquarter Units of
Brigades and Divisions that sometimes the officers are
embarked in one ship and the remainder of the personnel
in another. It appears advisable that one officer sgould
always remain with his Headquarter Unit. This will
obviate the recurrence of the difficulty alluded to,
by Captain H.C,Turner in his report attached.

Havre.   (sd) H.J.Bartholomew, Major.
23/3/15.   D.A.Q.M.G'

19th March, 1915.

Havre Base.

From,

Captain H.C.Turner, 2nd London Regt. "The Queens"
2nd London Division.

To,

The D.A.Q.M.G.

Havre Base.

Sir,

As senior officer in the party of 6 officers from the 2nd London Division who have been assisting in the disembarkation of the Division at Havre Base I have the honour to report that the movement of the Division has passed off without a hitch and that there has been no complaint excepting one as to which I aphend a separate report.

The arrangements made at the Base have worked well and every assistance has been given to Officers Commanding Units and trains by the Embarkation and Entraining Authorities.

All the Advance officers of the 2nd London Division are proceeding to rejoin their units today with the exception of Captain Molesly 21st Bn. London Regt. who is remaining in the Officers' Hospital.

I have the honour to be,

Sir,

Your obedient servant,

sd.H.C.Turner. Captain.

2nd Bn.London Regt. "The Queens".

Report on complaint by Lt-Col. Thwaites. C.S.O.

2nd London Division.

Havre,
19th March, 1915.

On Tuesday night March 16th on proceeding to Halle 3 at 7 pm to visit the troops of the 2nd London Division encamped there, to satisfy myself that all was well and all units provided with the necessary information and supplies and prepared for the next days movement, I found that the Headquarters Units of the 2nd London Division landed in the morning had not yet drawn their rations for the next day, had not indented for deficiencies or winter clothing and had no information as to their procedure on the next day.

I met various members of the Staff including Lt-Col. Thwaites and Lt-Col. Newton-Taylor (Commandant 2nd London Div.) who made complaint to me. I supplied them with all the required information and remained till the ration party had gone out and the Headquarters Quarter Master Sergeant had gone to indent for clothing etc.

I have to report that this occurrence was not so far as I can see in any way due to the neglect of the A.M.L.O. or their assistants but was due to the fact that the Headquarters, Personnel were divided on the boats and that no officer travelled with the personnel. The non-commissioned officer in charge reported that he had no deficiencies and did not wish to draw any winter clothing when he was approached by the A.M.L.O. about his indent.

The officers of the Divisional Headquarters disembarking separately failed to received the instructions due for the Headquarters Personnel.

sd. C.H. Turner, Captain. 2nd Bn. London. Regt.

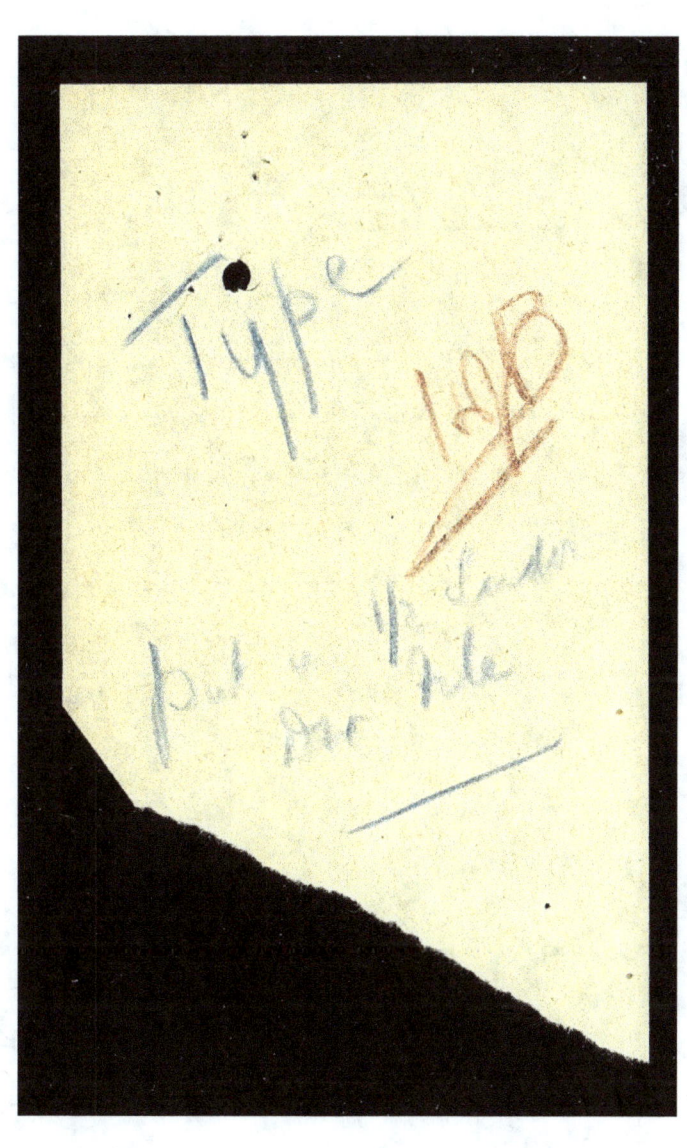

March 19. 1915.

Havre Base.

From Capt H. C. Turner. 2nd London Regt. "The Queen's"
2nd London Division. T.F.

To the D A Q M G. Havre Base.

Sir,

As senior officer of the party of 8 officers from the 2nd London Division who have been assisting in the disembarkation & entraining of the Division at Havre Base, I have the honour to report that the movement of the Division has passed off without a hitch & that there have been no complaints except one as to which I append a separate report.

The arrangements made at the Base have worked well & every assistance has been given to Officers Commanding Units & trains by the embarkation & entraining authorities.

All the advance officers of the 2nd London Division are proceeding to rejoin their units today with the exception of Captain Mobely 2nd Bn. The London Regt. who is remaining in the Officers Hospital.

I have the honour, Sir

Your obedient Servant

H. Charlewood Turner Captain
2nd Bn The London Regt.
"The Queen's"

Report on complaint by Lt Col Thwaites
C.S.O. 2nd London Division.

Hanne.
March 19. 1915.

On Tuesday night March 16 on proceeding
to Hallu III at 7 p.m. to visit the headqrs of
the 2nd London Division reached there to satisfy
myself that all was well & all units
provided with the necessary information &
supplies & prepared for the next day's movement,
I found that the Headquarters Unit of the
2nd London Division landed in the morning had
not yet drawn their rations for the next day,
had not indented for deficiencies on units Clothing
& had no information as to their procedure on
the next day.

I met various members of the Staff
including Lt Col Thwaites & Lt Col. Newton Taylor
(Commandant 2nd London Divn Hqrs) who made
complaint to me. I supplied them with
all the required information & remained till the
ration party had gone out & the Hqrs Quarter
Master Sergeant had gone to indent for Clothing Etc.

I have brought that this occurrence
was not so far as I can see in any way due
to the neglect of the A.M.L.O. or other division
but was due to the fact that the Headquarters
personnel were divided on the train & that
no Officer travelled with the personnel. The
non commissioned officer in charge reported that he
had no deficiencies & did not wish to draw
any deficiencies units Clothing when he was approached
by the A.M.L.O. about an indent.

The Officers of the Divisional Headquarters
disembarking separately failed to give the instructions
due for the Hdqrs personnel.

D.A.Q.M.G.

I forward a report on the transport of the 2nd.London Division.

Animals   Horses   The horses of this division were generally speaking of a very good stamp, but their condition was not as good as those of the North Midland Division. There were no mules with the regimental transport of infantry battalions, all animals with G.S.limbered wagons were light draft horses. In the case of the previous Division and with Territorial Infantry battalions arriving within the past month, there have invariably been a number of mules to replace light draft horses.

Shoeing   The shoeing was good. Units had shoes of varying sizes, and had their proper complement of cold shoers, farrier artificers, and farrier's tools.

Vehicles   All modern vehicles and in good order, except for certain exceptions where damage had occurred in transit. On one day seven vehicles were damaged. The damage consists of broken or bent footboards at the front of the wagon, damaged hand brakes at the rear. These parts of the vehicles were always knocked upwards, and I am strongly of opinion that it occurred when being lowered into the hold of the ship on embarkation.

Harness   All new P.D. G.S.Harness. From the fact that it was new, its strength was all that could be desired. But it was not in good condition for actual work, being hard and requiring dubbin. I ordered an extra supply of dubbin for every unit, and where they will use it, no harm will be done. At the same time all units now come out with new

(harness

harness, and it should be softened before hard work is undertaken.

I notice that in some instances horses were showing signs of galls from the breast harness when entraining. These galls were occasioned during the march from docks to camp, and from camp to entraining point.

Other Equipment

Every unit required horse rugs, and these were drawn. I do not think it necessary to continue this issue.

Mechanical Transport.

Very little mechanical transport arrived at this Base.

Motor cars for the Headquarter Staff and Divisional Train supply officers. All in good order; what spares necessary were issued.

The Signal Co. R.E. had 16 motor bicycles and 1 motor lorry.

The Sanitary Section had 1 motor lorry.

General Remarks

Nil.

Havre
24/3/15

Major
D.A.D.T., Base

Embarkation Commandant,
    Southampton.

****

With reference to the attached report from Captain Turner, 2nd Battalion, London Regt, Senior Disembarkation Officer, 2nd London Division, I would be glad if arrangements could be made in future to ensure that an officer of the Headquarters Units of the Division accompanies the Headquarter Personnel on the same ship.

The move of the 2nd London Division was carried out without a hitch with the exception of the contretemp allowed in Captain Turner's report, and this would have been avoided had an officer accompanied the Headquarter Personnel.

Havre,
23/3/15.

Brig. General,
Base Commandant.

CENTRAL REGISTRY.

Central No. and Date.
7185
23-3-15.

7185

SUBJECT.

Report on Disembarkation &c.
2nd London Division

Reference Files.

Referred to	Date	Referred to	Date	Referred to	Date
A	23.3.15				
Q	23/3				
a.					

Filed	Date

SCHEDULE OF CORRESPONDENCE.

Sub. No.	Date	To whom	PRÉCIS
	25/3	Embark Comndt S'hope	Necy arrangements c[...] to be made to [...] Officers of HQ & Units of the Div. accompanies [...] Personnel on the Same ship
	26/3	IGC.	Forwarding Reports

REPORT ON THE DISEMBARKATION OF THE 2nd LONDON
TERRITORIAL DIVISION.

The number of days of actual disembarking were seven.

An Infantry Brigade was sent over in advance arriving here on the 10th and 11th March. The remainder of the Division started to arrive on the 15th March and continued till the 18th March when there was an interval of two days, and on the 21st the Divisional Ammunition Column arrived so that the actual time that it took to complete the Division over here was eleven days.

I understand that the Divisional Ammunition Column was detained in England to be equipped with fresh horses as the original ones had contracted mange.

All units were sent up to the Rest Camp on arrival with the exception of the Divisional Ammunition Column and owing to high water being at an early hour in the morning the Artillery and Regimental Transport of practically all units were able to get up to Camp before dark.

The small "butterfly" boats were all berthed at the Quai d'Escale, and on one day as many as nine of these boats were berthed there at once. The whole of these were cleared and sailed in about two hours after the disembarkation commenced.

I consider that the practice of sending the bulk of the troops over on these ships most satisfactory. They are disembarked at 7.0 a.m. each morning and the troops are up in Camp early in the day.

With regard to the Divisional Ammunition Column their horses were issued to them at the last minute no harness having been fitted at all. In spite of this and

-2-

being rather short of time they were at their entraining point at the time ordered which I think was a very good performance and reflects credit on the unit.

The usual temporary A.M.L.O.s were sent over and they all were keen on their work and were very useful especially Captain J.W.Pace, 24th London Regiment whose services were a great benefit.

I attach a list of the ships that arrived with time table, etc. All the ships were berthed at the Quays as requested, and in very good time.

Havre.   Major.
22/3/15.   M.L.O.

RECORD OF TRANSPORT FOR 2nd LONDON DIVISION.

Name of ship.	Hour due.	Hour reported in the Roads.	Hour entering Port.	Hour berthed.	Hour discharged.	Name of Quay.	Remarks.
March 10th:-							
Viper.	4.30 a.m.		4.10 a.m.	4.35 a.m.	8.45 a.m.	Escale.	
Copenhagen.	4.15 "		5.45 "	4.15 "	8.0 "	"	
Queen Alexandra.	5.0 "		5.50 "	4.30 "	8.30 "	"	
Trafford Hall.	5.0 "		5.20 "	6.5 "	12.15 noon	Plata O	
Rossetti.	5.0 "		4.5 "	4.30 "	12.30 "	Pondicherry	
Duchess of Argyll.	4.0 "		3.20 "	4.0 "	7.40 a.m.	Escale.	
March 11th:-							
Munich.	1.30 a.m.		1.50 a.m.	2.30 a.m.	7.45 a.m.	Escale.	
Empress Queen.	1.50 "		2.0 "	2.30 "	7.45 "	"	
Courtfield.	5.0 "		5.30 "	4.15 "	11.40 "	Pondicherry.	
March 15th:-							
Copenhagen.	3.30 a.m.		3.30 a.m.	6.20 a.m.	8.15 a.m.	Escale.	
Viper.	3.30 "		3.30 "	4.0 "	8.15 "	"	
Mount Temple.	5.0 "	6.30 a.m.	8.30 "	10.0 "	4.5 p/m.	Pondicherry.	
Trafford Hall.	5.30 "	6.30 "	8.30 "	10.0 "	5.0 "	Plata O.	
City of Dunkirk.	6.30 "	6.30 "	8.30 "	10.0 "	4.30 "	Pondicherry.	
March 16th:-							
Empress Queen.	1.30 a.m.	5.0 a.m.	5.40 a.m.	4.0 a.m.	8.15 a.m	Escale.	
Munich.	1.30 "	5.0 "	3.40 "	4.0 "	8.30 "	"	
Anglo Canadian.	5.30 "	5.30 "	9.15 "	10.0 "	5.0 p.m	Pondicherry.	
Chyebassa.	4.0 "	4.0 "	9.15 "	10.15 "	5.50 "	"	
Matheran.	4.0 "	5.30 "	9.0 "	10.0 "	4.30 "	Plata O.	

Name of ship.	Hour due.	Hour reported in the Roads.	Hour entering Port.	Hour berthed.	Hour discharged.	Name of Quay.	Remarks.
March 17th:-							
Queen Alexandra.	1.0 a.m.		1.0 a.m.	1.30 a.m.	7.45 a.m.	Escale.	
Inventor.	4.30 "	6.30 a.m.	9.30 "	10.30 "	4.15 p.m.	Pondichery.	
Architect.	4.30 "	8.0 "	9.30 "	10.15 "	5.10 "	"	
March 18th:-							
Marguerite.	2.0 a.m.		3.30 a.m.	4.0 a.m.	8.30 a.m.	Escale.	
Duchess of Montrose	3.0 "		4.30 "	4.50 "	8.0 "	"	
Empress Queen.	2.30 "		4.0 "	4.30 "	8.15 "	"	
Jupiter.			4.30 "	5.0 "	9.30 "	"	
Belmoral.			4.55 "	5.30 "	8.50 "	"	
Atlanta.			5.0 "	5.35 "	8.0 "	"	
Blackwell.	4.0 "	0.30 a.m	10.45 "	11.15 "	0.0 p.n	Plata O.	
Courfield.	4.0 "	8.30 "	10.35 "	11.50 "	5.10 "	Pondichery.	
City of Chester	5.30 "	8.50 "	11.0 "	noon	4.30 "	Pondichery.	
March 21st:-							
Empress Queen.	1.30 a.m.		1.30 a.m.	2.0 a.m.	8.10 a.m	Escale.	
Caledonian.	5.0 "	6.30 a.m.	11.30 "	12.30 p.m.	4.45 p.m.	Pondichery.	
Archimedes.	5.0 "	6.30 "	10.30 "	11.40 a.m.	5.0 "	"	

REPORT ON THE DISEMBARKATION OF THE 2nd LONDON
TERRITORIAL DIVISION.

The number of days of actual disembarking were seven.

An Infantry Brigade was sent over in advance arriving here on the 10th and 11th March. The remainder of the Division started to arrive on the 15th March and continued till the 18th March when there was an interval of two days, and on the 21st the Divisional Ammunition Column arrived so that the actual time that it took to complete the Division over here was eleven days.

I understand that the Divisional Ammunition Column was detained in England to be equipped with fresh horses as the original ones had contracted mange.

All units were sent up to the Rest Camp on arrival with the exception of the Divisional Ammunition Column and owing to high water being at an early hour in the morning the Artillery and Regimental Transport of practically all units were able to get up to Camp before dark.

The small "butterfly" boats were all berthed at the Quai d'Escale, and on one day as many as nine of these boats were berthed there at once. The whole of these were cleared and sailed in about two hours after the disembarkation commenced.

I consider that the practice of sending the bulk of the troops over on these ships most satisfactory. They are disembarked at 7.0 a.m. each morning and the troops are up in Camp early in the day.

With regard to the Divisional Ammunition Column their horses were issued to them at the last minute no harness having been fitted at all. In spite of this and

-2-

being rather short of time they were at their entraining point at the time ordered which I think was a very good performance and reflects credit on the unit.

The usual temporary A.M.L.O.s were sent over and they all were keen on their work and were very useful especially Captain J.W.Pace, 24th London Regiment whose services were a great benefit.

I attach a list of the ships that arrived with time table, etc. All the ships were berthed at the Quays as requested, and in very good time.

Havre.   Major.
22/5/15.   M.L.O.

RECORD OF TRANSPORT FOR 2nd LONDON DIVISION.

Name of ship.	Hour due.	Hour reported in the Roads.	Hour entering Port.	Hour berthed.	Hour discharged.	Name of Quay.	Remarks.
March 10th:-							
Viper.	4.30 a.m.		4.10 a.m.	4.55 a.m.	6.45 a.m.	Escale.	
Copenhagen.	4.15 "		5.45 "	4.15 "	8.0 "	"	
Queen Alexandra.	5.0 "		5.50 "	4.50 "	9.50 "	"	
Trafford Hall.	5.0 "		5.20 "	6.5 "	12.15 noon	Plate G	
Rossetti.	3.0 "		4.5 "	4.30 "	12.30 "	Pondichery.	
Duchess of Argyll.	4.0 "		5.30 "	4.0 "	7.40 a.m.	Escale.	
March 11th:-							
Munich.	1.30 a.m.		1.50 a.m.	2.30 a.m.	7.45 a.m.	Escale.	
Empress Queen.	1.50 "		2.0 "	3.30 "	7.45 "	"	
Courtfield.	3.0 "		3.30 "	4.15 "	11.40 "	Pondichery.	
March 15th:-							
Copenhagen.	5.30 a.m.		5.30 a.m.	6.20 a.m.	8.15 a.m.	Escale.	
Viper.	5.30 "		5.50 "	4.0 "	8.15 "	"	
Mount Temple.	5.0 "	6.30 a.m.	5.0 "	10.0 "	4.5 p.m.	Pondichery.	
Trafford Hall.	5.30 "	6.30 "	6.30 "	10.0 "	5.0 "	Plate O.	
City of Dunkirk.	5.30 "	6.30 "	6.30 "	10.0 "	4.30 "	Pondichery.	
March 16th:-							
Empress Queen.	1.30 a.m.	3.0 a.m.	3.40 a.m.	4.0 a.m.	8.15 a.m.	Escale.	
Munich.	1.30 "	3.0 "	3.40 "	4.0 "	8.30 "	"	
Anglo Canadian.	5.30 "	8.30 "	9.15 "	10.0 "	5.0 p.m.	Pondichery.	
Cagabaana.	4.0 "	4.0 "	9.15 "	10.15 "	5.50 "	"	
Esthoren.	4.0 "	5.30 "	9.0 "	10.0 "	4.30 "	Plate O.	

Name of ship.	Hour due.	Hour reported in entering the Roads.	Hour berthed.	Hour discharged.	Name of Quay.	Remarks.
March 17th:-						
Susan Alexandra.	1.0 a.m.		1.30 a.m.	7.45 a.m.	Escale.	
Inventor.	4.30 "	6.30 a.m.	10.20 "	4.15 p.m.	Pondichery.	
Architect.	4.30 "	8.0 "	10.15 "	5.10 "	"	
March 18th:-						
Margaerite.	2.0 a.m.		4.0 a.m.	8.30 a.m.	Escale.	
Duchess of Montrae	3.0 "		4.30 "	6.0 "	"	
Myrean Queen.	2.30 "		4.30 "	8.15 "	"	
Jupiter.			5.0 "	9.30 "	"	
Mallard.			5.30 "	8.55 "	"	
Atlanta.			5.55 "	6.0 "	"	
Blackwell.	4.0 "	6.30 a.m	11.15 "	0.0 p.m	Plata O.	
Courtfield.	4.0 "	8.30 "	11.30 "	5.10 "	Pondichery.	
City of Chester.	5.30 "	9.30 "	noon	4.30 "	Pondichery.	
March 21st:-						
Empress Queen.	1.30 a.m.		2.0 a.m.	8.10 a.m	Escale.	
Caledonia.	5.0 "	6.30 a.m.	12.30 p.m.	4.45 p.m.	Pondichery.	
Archimedes.	5.0 "	6.30 "	11.40 a.m.	5.0 "	"	

REPORT ON THE DISEMBARKATION OF THE 2nd LONDON
TERRITORIAL DIVISION.

The number of days of actual disembarking were seven.

An Infantry Brigade was sent over in advance arriving here on the 10th and 11th March. The remainder of the Division started to arrive on the 15th March and continued till the 18th March when there was an interval of two days, and on the 21st the Divisional Ammunition Column arrived so that the actual time that it took to complete the Division over here was eleven days.

I understand that the Divisional Ammunition Column was detained in England to be equipped with fresh horses as the original ones had contracted mange.

All units were sent up to the Rest Camp on arrival with the exception of the Divisional Ammunition Column and owing to high water being at an early hour in the morning the Artillery and Regimental Transport of practically all units were able to get up to Camp before dark.

The small "butterfly" boats were all berthed at the Quai d'Escale, and on one day as many as nine of these boats were berthed there at once. The whole of these were cleared and sailed in about two hours after the disembarkation commenced.

I consider that the practice of sending the bulk of the troops over on these ships most satisfactory. They are disembarked at 7.0 a.m. each morning and the troops are up in Camp early in the day.

With regard to the Divisional Ammunition Column their horses were issued to them at the last minute no harness having been fitted at all. In spite of the

-2-

being rather short of time they were at their entraining point at the time ordered which I think was a very good performance and reflects credit on the unit.

The usual temporary A.M.L.O.s were sent over and they all were keen on their work and were very useful especially Captain J.W.Pace, 24th London Regiment whose services were a great benefit.

I attach a list of the ships that arrived with time table, etc. All the ships were berthed at the Quays as requested, and in very good time.

Havre.   Major.
22/3/18.   M.L.O.

RECORD OF TRANSPORT FOR 2nd LONDON DIVISION.

Name of Ship.	Hour Gas-masks unpacked-in-readiness.	Hour reported in entering the Roads.	Hour entering Fort.	Hour berthed.	Hour discharged.	Name of Quay.	Remarks.
March 10th:-							
Piper.	4.30 a.m.		4.30 a.m.	5.35 a.m.	6.45 a.m.	Escale.	
Copenhagen.	4.15 "		3.45 "	4.15 "	8.0 "	"	
Queen Alexandra.	5.0 "		5.30 "	6.30 "	8.30 "	"	
Trafford Hall.	5.0 "		5.30 "	6.5 "	10.15 noon	Plate O	
Lanatti.	5.0 "		4.5 "	4.30 "	10.30 "	Pondicherry	
Duchess of Argyll.	4.0 "		3.30 "	4.0 "	7.40 a.m.	Escale	
March 11th:-							
Munich.	1.30 a.m.		1.50 a.m.	2.30 a.m.	7.45 a.m.	Escale.	
Empress Queen.	1.30 "		2.0 "	2.50 "	7.45 "	"	
Courtfield.	5.0 "		5.30 "	4.15 "	11.40 "	Pondicherry.	
March 12th:-							
Jerusalem.	5.30 a.m.		5.50 a.m.	6.30 a.m.	8.15 a.m.	Escale.	
Viper.	5.30 "		5.30 "	4.0 "	8.15 "	"	
Earl Lonsdale.	5.0 "	6.30 a.m.	6.30 "	10.0 "	4.0 p.m.	Pondicherry.	
Trafford Hall.	5.30 "	6.30 "	8.30 "	10.0 "	5.0 "	Plate O.	
City of Dunkirk.	5.30 "	6.30 "	8.30 "	10.0 "	4.30 "	Pondicherry.	
March 13th:-							
Queen Mary.	1.30 a.m.		5.40 a.m.	4.0 a.m.	8.15 a.m.	Escale.	
Ionia.	1.30 "		5.45 "	4.0 "	8.30 "	"	
Africa Venetian.	3.30 "		5.15 "	10.0 "	5.0 p.m.	Pondicherry.	
Copenhagen.	4.0 "		5.15 "	10.15 "	4.30 "	"	
Ratesan.	4.0 "		5.30 "	10.0 "	4.30 "	Plate O.	

Name of Ship.	Hour due.	Hour reported in entering the Roads.	Hour Port.	Hour berthed.	Hour discharged.	Name of Quay.	Remarks.
March 17th:-							
Queen Alexandra.	1.0 a.m.		1.0 a.m.	1.30 a.m.	7.45 a.m.	Escale.	
Investor.	4.30 "	6.30 a.m.	6.50 "	10.30 "	4.15 p.m.	Pondichery.	
Architect.	4.30 "	8.0 "	8.30 "	10.10 "	5.10 "	"	
March 18th:-							
Marguerite.	2.0 a.m.		3.30 a.m.	4.0 a.m.	6.30 a.m.	Escale.	
Duchess of Montrose	3.0 "		4.30 "	4.30 "	8.0 "	"	
Empress Queen.	3.30 "		4.0 "	4.30 "	6.15 "	"	
Jupiter.			4.30 "	5.0 "	8.30 "	"	
Balmoral.			4.55 "	5.30 "	8.30 "	"	
Atlanta.			5.0 "	5.30 "	8.0 "	"	
Bluebell.	4.0 "	6.30 a.m	10.45 "	11.15 "	6.0 p.m	Plots G.	
Courtfield.	4.0 "	8.30 "	10.55 "	11.50 "	5.10 "	Pondichery.	
City of Chester.	5.30 "	8.30 "	11.0 "	noon	4.30 "	Pondichery.	
March 21st:-							
Empress Queen.	1.30 a.m.		1.30 a.m.	2.0 a.m.	3.10 a.m.	Escale.	
Caledonian.	5.0 "	6.30 a.m.	11.30 "	12.30 p.m.	4.45 p.m.	Pondichery.	
Archimedes.	5.0 "	6.30 "	10.30 "	11.40 a.m.	5.0 "	"	

Report on the Disembarking of
the 2nd London Territorial Division.

The number of actual days of Disembarking
were seven.

An Infantry Brigade was sent
over in advance arriving here on the 10th
and 11th March. The remainder of
the Division started to arrive
on the 15th March and continued
till the 18th March; when there were
two days
interval the 19th & 20th.
and on the 21st
The Divisional Ammunition Column
arrived.

So that the actual time that
it took to complete the Division
was eleven days
I understand that the Divisional
Ammunition Column was
detained

in Endeavour to fully Equipped with
fresh horses, as the original
ones had contracted mange.
All units were sent up to the
Rest Camp on arrival, with the exception of the Divisional
owing to the high water being at an
Early hour in the morning, the Artillery
Regiment, & practically all Units,
and Transport, were able to get
up to Camp before dark —
The small "butterfly" boats were
all discharged berthed at the Quaie
d'Escale, & in one day as many
as nine of these boats were
berthed there at once. The whole
of these were cleared & sailed in
about two hours after the
disembarkation commenced.

I consider that the practice of sending the bulk of the troops over in their ships most satisfactory. They are disembarked at 7 A.M. each morning and the troops are up in Camp early in the day. With regard to the Divisional Ammunition Column, their horses were issued to them at the last minute, no harness having been fitted at all. In spite of this, as being rather short of time, they were at their entraining point at the time ordered, which I think was a very good performance and reflects credit on the Reserve the Horse Company. A. R. Hos
—
3

well often over. and they all
were keen on their work. and were
of great assistance. ~~and~~ especially
      (very useful)
Captain J.W. Pace 24th Lada Regt horse
carried were a great benefit.
I attach a list of the ships that
arrived with horses hales &ca
all the ships were berthed, at the
Quays. as requested, and in very
good time.

                    C.G. Humphreys
                       Major RAO
Havre
22.iii.15

NOT TO BE WRITTEN ON.

"C" Form (Original).   Army Form C.2123.

MESSAGES AND SIGNALS.

Prefix	Code	Words 77	Received From	Sent, or sent out At ... m.	Office Stamp
Charges to collect	£ s. d.		By	To	
Service Instructions.				By	

Handed in at **AGO** Office ... m. Received ... m.

TO   One Ldn Divn

Sender's Number	Day of Month	In reply to Number	AAA
G 448	23rd		

Reference yours G/2/1 6th 7th and 8th Battns are to be prepared to march to BETHUNE tomorrow starting not before 2 pm preparatory to going into trenches evening 25th under arrangements to be made by Brigade of 2nd Divn AAA 2nd Divn will arrange to billet these Battns in BETHUNE AAA Further details will be sent in morning AAA Addressed 2nd LONDON Div repeated 2nd Divn

FROM PLACE & TIME   1st Corps   9.55 pm

MESSAGES AND SIGNALS.

TO: Fourth Lon. Inf. Bde

Sender's Number: G.15
Day of Month: 23/3
AAA

1st Corps wire commences 6th 7th and 8th Battalions will be prepared to march to BETHUNE tomorrow 24th instant not before 2 pm preparatory to going into trenches evening of 25th under arrangements to be made by Brigade of 2nd Division aaa 2nd Division will arrange to billet these Battalions in BETHUNE aaa. Further details will be sent in morning aaa Addressed 2nd London Division repeated 2nd Division aaa ends. aaa Warn Battalions tonight. aaa Acknowledge.

From: Second Lon. Div.
Time: 11-10 pm

"A" Form. Army Form C. 2121.

MESSAGES AND SIGNALS.

TO: 2 London Div⁻

Sender's Number	Day of Month	In reply to Number	
S.C. 37	24/3/15	G. 18	AAA

Your message number as above received AAA

From: Fourth Lon. Inf. Bde.

Place

Time: 12.15 am

1ST ARMY CORPS
GENERAL STAFF
(OPERATIONS SECTION)
No. 251/G/.
Date

2nd Division.
2nd London Division.

The 6th, 7th and 8th London Battalions will proceed to BETHUNE this afternoon. Each of these battalions will be temporarily attached to one of the brigades of 2nd Division, and will do duty in the front line under arrangements to be made by the G.O.C. the infantry brigade concerned. These arrangements should provide for each company in each of the three battalions undertaking a tour of 24 hours in the trenches themselves. As soon as a battalion has completed this tour it will return to its billets in the 2nd London Division area. The 1st Corps and 2nd London Division are to be kept informed of the daily progress.

10.30 A.M.
24th March, 1915.

Brig. General.
S.G.S.O., 1st Corps.

2nd London Division.
===================

The 6th, 7th, and 8th London Battalions will proceed to BETHUNE this afternoon. Each of these battalions will be temporarily attached to one of the brigades of the 2nd Division, and will do duty in the front line under arrangements to be made by the G.O.C. the infantry Brigade concerned. These arrangements should provide for each company in each of the three battalions undertaking a tour of 24 hours in the trenches themselves. As soon as a battalion has completed this tour it will return to its billets in the 2nd London Division Area. The 1st Corps and 2nd London Division are to be kept informed of the daily progress.

No.251/G.
24/3/15.

(sd) R.Whigham, Br.Genl.
S.G.S.O., 1st Corps.

(2)

G.O.C.,
  4th Lon.Inf.Bde.
=====================

For necessary action and retention please.

Kindly acknowledge receipt.

2 L.Div.G/2/2
24th March 1915.

Lt.Colonel
General Staff,
2nd London Division, T.F.

Headquarters - 2nd London Division.

1. Your No. 2.L. Div. G/2/2 dated 24th March 1915, re move of three Battalions to BETHUNE, received.

G. Cuthbert
Brig. General.
C-dg 4th London Inf. Brigade.

B.M. 47.
24/3/15.

Sr. Ed. Rosales
á
Aug. Kaulbs.
H. m.
26.3.15.

4th (Guards) Brigade.
5th Infy. Brigade.
6th Infy. Brigade.

2nd DIVISION
GENERAL STAFF
No. G.S. 304/1
Date 25/3/15

....

The period of time for which battalions of 2nd London Division will be attached to the infantry brigades of this division has not been defined. It will not however, be less than 6 days as far as the 6th, 7th, and 8th City of London battalions are concerned.

2. Brigade Commanders must however bear in mind that the whole of the 2nd London Division requires to gain as quickly as possible experience of the conditions of warfare now obtaining in our front. The instruction of any one battalion must therefore not be prolonged beyond what is necessary to give every portion of it a short experience of the duties of a unit in front line.

3. The G.O.C. suggests that each platoon shall do 24 hours in the trenches with regular troops, 24 hours in support, and the remainder of the time in reserve. That part of the battalion which is in reserve may be employed for digging, or for other necessary work, and the whole battalion should be usefully employed daily.

4. If time and circumstances permit, it is advisable that after the completion of platoon training, each company should take its place in the trenches as a whole.

5. On the assumption that 2 platoons can be accommodated daily in the firing line, it is calculated that the whole period of training for a battalion will last from 8 - 12 days.

(sd) Louis Vaughan

25th March 1915.
Lieut-Colonel.
General Staff. 2nd Division.

2.

2nd London Division.

For information.

25/3/15.
Major-General.
Commanding 2nd Division.

4th (Guards) Brigade.
5th Infy.Brigade.
6th Infy.Brigade.
===========================

The period of time for which battalions of the 2nd London Division will be attached to the infantry brigades of this division has not been defined. It will not, however, be less than 8 days as far as the 6, 7th and 8th City of London Battalions are concerned.

2. Brigade Commanders must however bear in mind that the whole of the 2nd London Division requires to gain as quickly as possible experience of the conditions of warfare now obtaining in our front. The instruction of any one battalion must therefore not be prolonged beyond what is necessary to give every portion of it a short experience of the duties of a unit in front line.

3. The G.O.C. suggests that each platoon shall do 24 hours in the trenches with regular troops, 24 hours in support, and the remainder of the time in reserve. That part of the battalion which is in reserve may be employed for digging, or for other necessary work, and the whole battalion should be usefully employed daily.

4. If time and circumstances permit, it is advisable that after the completion of platoon training, each company should take its place in the trenches as a whole.

5. On the assumption that 2 platoons can be accommodated daily in the firing line, it is calculated that the whole period of training for a battalion will last from 8 - 12 days.

(sd) L. Vaughan, Lt.Colonel,
General Staff,
2nd Division.

23/3/15.

(2)

2nd London Division.
===========================

For information.

No.304/1/G.S.
25/3/15.

(sd) H.S.Horne, Maj.Genl.
Comdg. 2nd Division.

(3)

4.5.6 th Lon.Inf.Bde.
===========================

For information and retention.

(sd) [signature]

Lt.Colonel,
General Staff,
2nd London Division T.F.

2 Lon.Div.G/2/3.

26th March 1915.

"A" Form.
MESSAGES AND SIGNALS. Army Form C. 2121.

TO: 2 Lon Div

Sender's Number: G 467
Day of Month: 25
AAA

1st Div will not be ready to take units of your Div for some days but will take Officers and NCO's AAA How many Officers and NCO's do you wish to send from A. Bde at a time.

From: 1st Corps
Time: 9-45 pm

"A" Form.   Army Form C. 2121.
MESSAGES AND SIGNALS.   No. of Message_____

Prefix____ Code____ m.	Words.	Charge.	This message is on a/c of:	Recd. at____ m.
Office of Origin and Service Instructions.				Date____
	Sent			
	At____ m.		____Service.	From____
	To____			
	By____		(Signature of "Franking Officer.")	By____

| TO | 5 | Lon | Inf. | Bde. |
| | | | | |

| Sender's Number | Day of Month | In reply to Number | |
| * G.T. 27. | 25 | | AAA |

1st	Corps	wire	begins	AAA
1st	Div	will	not	be
ready	to	take	units	of
your	Div	for	some	days
but	will	take	Officers	and
NCO's	aaa	How	many	Officers
and	NCO's	do	you	wish
to	send	from	a	Bde
at	a	time	aaa	ends
aaa	Send	in	at	once
number	of	Officers	and	NCO's
available	to	send		

From Second   Lon   Div
Place
Time 10-4 am

"A" Form.　　　　　　　　　　Army Form C. 2121.
MESSAGES AND SIGNALS.　　No. of Message _____

Prefix ___ Code ___ m.	Words.	Charge.	This message is on a/c of:	Recd. at ___ m.
Office of Origin and Service Instructions.	Sent			Date ___
	At ___ m.		_____ Service.	From ___
	To ___			
	By ___		(Signature of "Franking Officer.")	By ___

TO { Second Lon Div

Sender's Number	Day of Month	In reply to Number	
Bm. 90	25"	G.T. 27	AAA

Thirty Officers Thirty five NCO's
Thirty Two.

(pencil annotation: 2½ Div G 1-28 11-30 pm)

From　5　Lon.　Inf.　Bde.
Place
Time　11-10 pm

The above may be forwarded as now corrected.　(Z)

"A" Form.   Army Form C. 2121.

MESSAGES AND SIGNALS.   No. of Message_____

| TO | 1st | Corps. | | |

Sender's Number	Day of Month	In reply to Number	AAA
G.28	26	G.467	

	Following	number	available	are
Officers	35.	NCOs.	32	

From: 2nd Lon Div
Place:
Time: 8.45 am

"A" Form. Army Form C. 2121.
MESSAGES AND SIGNALS.

TO: Second Lon. Div.

Sender's Number: Cy 476. Day of Month: 26th AAA

Two	Motor	busses	will	be
sent	out	Sunday	28th	to
take	six	Officers	and	six
NCOs	to	Hd Qrs	2nd	Inf.
Bde.	at	CSE DU RAUX	N
of.	LOISNE	and	nine	Officers
and	nine	NCOs	to	3rd
Inf.	Bde	at	RICHEBOURG ST
VAAST	aaa	Both	Parties	will
arrive	at	destination	3 pm	aaa
Further	instructions	will	be	sent
later. aaa	Address	2nd	London
Repeated	1st	Division

From: 1st Corps
Time: 10.20 pm

"A" Form. Army Form C. 2121.

MESSAGES AND SIGNALS. No. of Message_____

Prefix___ Code___ m.	Words.	Charge.	This message is on a/c of:	Recd. at___ m.
Office of Origin and Service Instructions.	Sent At___ m. To___ By___		___Service. (Signature of "Franking Officer.")	Date___ From___ By___

TO { 5 | Lon. | Inf. | Bde

Sender's Number	Day of Month	In reply to Number	
G.34	27"		AAA

Two Motor Buses will be sent out Sunday 28th to take six Officers and six NCO's to Hd. Qrs 2nd Inf Bde at CSE DU RAUX N of LOISNE and nine Officers and nine NCO's to 3rd Inf Bde Hd. Qrs. at RICHEBOURG ST VAAST aaa Both parties will arrive at destination at 3 pm aaa Further instructions will be sent later

From _____ Div
Place
Time 7-50 am

The above may be forwarded as now corrected. (Z)

Censor._____ Signature of Addressor or person authorised to telegraph in his name
* This line should be erased if not required.

1st Corps H Qrs.
27·3·15

Dear Thwaites

Gen. Whigham asked me to write to you about the attachment of your Infy. to 1st & 2nd Divns.

The 3 Battns. now with 2nd Division will remain 8 to 12 days, when they will be succeeded by 3 more and so on.

The 1st Division will not be able to take Battns. for several days, but can go on taking officers & N.C.Os.

The party that goes up tomorrow (Sunday) will return on Monday when another similar party can go up, and so on, as long as you wish.

We have asked for 2 motor busses to be here at 10 a.m. tomorrow, but no answer has yet been received. They will return in the evening, ready to take up another party on Monday & to bring back the first party.

We hope to send all your battns. up in time, and the extra 24 hours experience of some of the officers & N.C.Os. will not be all to the good. But it won't be necessary to send any who have been up with their battns. for the 24 hours business.

Yours sincerely
Hereward Wake

Dealt with G 42 MMM

Wt. W1154/2240. 9/11. 7,500,000. Sch. 4a.   "A" Form.   Army Form C. 2121.

MESSAGES AND SIGNALS.   No. of Message_____

Prefix ____ Code ____ m.	Words	Charge	This message is on a/c of:	Recd. at _____ m.
Office of Origin and Service Instructions.	Sent			Date _____
_____	At _____ m.		_____ Service.	From _____
_____	To _____			
_____	By _____		(Signature of "Franking Officer.")	By _____

TO	5th	Lon.	Inf.	Bde.

Sender's Number.	Day of Month	In reply to Number	
G.42.	27th		AAA

Ref. G.34 of today aaa. The party of Officers and NCO's going to 1st Division on 28th will return on 29th when another party of similar strength is to go aaa. These parties each being away for 24 hours will be continued until all available have been up aaa. Report two days before your last party goes in order that another brigade may be warned aaa. Busses will NOT be available before 11 am tomorrow and you will be informed of actual time aaa. Busses will fetch Mondays party about the same time and bring back Sundays party on Monday afternoon aaa all parties will take rations with them.

From	Second	Lon.	Div
Place			
Time	3-30 p.m.		

The above may be forwarded as now corrected.   (Z)

_____ Censor.   Signature of Addressor or person authorised to telegraph in his name.

* This line should be erased if not required.

MESSAGES AND SIGNALS.

Army Form C. 2121.
"A" Form.

TO: 2nd Lon Div

Sender's Number: G.484
Day of Month: 27th
AAA

Reference 1st Corps G.476 Both parties should now reach destination 6 pm and not 3 pm as previously arranged

From: 1st Corps
Time: 6-20 pm

"A" Form.   Army Form C. 2121.

MESSAGES AND SIGNALS.

TO: Fifth Lon Inf Bde

Sender's Number: G 44
Day of Month: Twenty seventh
AAA

Reference my G.42 aaa first Corps wires that both parties should now reach destination 6 pm NOT 3 pm as previously arranged

From: Second Lon Div
Time: 7-4 pm

H.R. Hunt Capt GS

"A" Form.   Army Form C. 2121.

MESSAGES AND SIGNALS.

TO: Fifth Lon Inf Bde

Day of Month: Twenty eighth

AAA

Reference my C.94 of Twenty seventh aaa Two busses will arrive ~~at~~ BURBURE 4.30 pm today to convey parties to Second and Third Infantry Brigade aaa Please arrange for parties to meet Busses at Junction LILLERS road.

From: Second Lon Div
Time: 10-33 am

Russell   Church

No[?] .... atjoins LA COUTURE [?] 5.45 [?] [?]
.... [?] .... met by representative of
3rd BDE   We will take party up to H.Q.

No3 [?]   Going to 2nd BDE at CENSE DU
RAUX just East of LE TOURET map sq X.16
Party will be met by representative of 2nd BDE
Bus to arrive 5.45 pm. No transport will
be given to parties. Only to carry
...... kit as they can carry in the
trenches.
As far as road junction at LE TOURET only
not as far as CENSE DU RAUX

"A" Form.   Army Form C. 2121.

MESSAGES AND SIGNALS.

| TO | 5th | London | Inf | Bde. |

| Sender's Number | Day of Month | In reply to Number | AAA |
| G 50 | Twenty eighth | | |

Reference my S/48 number one bus containing six officers and six NCOs will be met at LA COUTURE CHURCH at 5.45 pm by representative of 3rd Brigade who will take party to the OP AAA Number two bus with remainder of party will be met by representative second Bde. at Road junction at LE TOURET Map square X.16 at 5.45 pm AAA thenceforth will proceed on foot to CENSE DU RAUX AAA No transport available parties will take such kit only as they can carry themselves to the trenches AAA acknowledge

From   Inf   London   Div
Place
Time   11.45 a.m.

Officer Commanding

2nd Lon.Div.Cyclist Compy.
================================

    Please detail an intelligent N.C.O. to report to this office at 11-30 a.m. this morning, to receive instructions to proceed to the Headquarters 1st Army Corps at 3-30 p.m. to guide two motor busses thence to BURBURE.

                                               H.R. Hunt

                                                        Captain,

                                                    General Staff,

                                      2nd London Division T.F.

Headquarters
2nd London Division

No 4/8 Sejt. Moyes W.G. will report in accordance with above instructions

28/3/1915
                             J. Clemens
                                 Captain
                                 Cyclist Co.

Headquarters

1st Corps.
================================

    Reference your message this morning, the above named N.C.O. is sent to guide the two motor busses to BURBURE.

                                               H.R. Hunt

                                                Captain,

                                          General Staff

                                  2nd London Division.

MESSAGES AND SIGNALS.

Army Form C. 2121.

TO: 5 Lon. Inf. Bde.

Sender's Number: G.54
Day of Month: 29th

Ref my G.48 & 50 of 28th Aug Busses will be at BURBURE at 10.30pm daily today and following days until attachments from your Brigade have been completed aaa Distribution of Parties and destination will be similar to those of yesterday aaa on arrival at destination busses will await arrival of previous days parties and return with them to Brigade Area aaa Acknowledge.

From: 2. Lon. D.2
Time: 10.12 am

"A" Form. Army Form C. 2121.

MESSAGES AND SIGNALS.   No. of Message_____

| Prefix___ Code___ m. | Words. | Charge. | This message is on a/c of: | Recd. at___ m. |
| Office of Origin and Service Instructions. | Sent At___ m. To___ By___ | | _____ Service. (Signature of "Franking Officer.") | Date___ From___ By___ |

TO { Fifth | Lon | Inf | Bde

Sender's Number	Day of Month	In reply to Number	AAA
	Ref	my	G 24 of
19th aaa	additional NCO	Arrange for	one
each	to	proceed	with
to ensure	Motor	bus	daily
bring back	its	waiting	to
aaa Busses	previous	days	party
in BURBURE	will	be	parked
acknowledge		during	day aaa

From	Seward	Lon	Div
Place			
Time	9 am		

The above may be forwarded as now corrected. (Z) H.R. ___ Capt

Censor.   Signature of Addressor or person authorised to telegraph in his name

* This line should be erased if not required.
(24473). M.R.Co.,Ltd. Wt.W4843/541. 50,000. 9/14. Forms C2121/10.

"A" Form. Army Form C. 2121.
MESSAGES AND SIGNALS.

TO 1st Corps

Sender's Number	Day of Month	In reply to Number	
C1/29	26th	257(G)	AAA

Presume intended that Section Brigade
Ammunition Column accompanies 5" Howitzer
Battery and portion of Divisional
Ammunition Column carry ~~ammunition~~ 5"
ammunition

From Second Lon. Div.
Place
Time 9.30 A.M.

"C" Form (Duplicate). Army Form C. 2123.
MESSAGES AND SIGNALS.   No. of Message M.31

Charges to Pay. Office Stamp.
£   s.   d.

Service Instructions.

Handed in at ACO   Office   m. Received   m.

TO 2nd Lieut Dumas

Sender's Number	Day of Month	In reply to Number	AAA
Hy 165	26th		

Air Reports this morning shows no unusual movement opposite joint corps front nor in area FROMELLES AUBERS ILLIES HERLIES AAA Second Army Report no movement of importance AAA Trains were reported by our advanced trenches in GIVENCHY Section to be very active round LA BASSEE between 8.15 pm and 9.30 pm last night AAA FESTUBERT ---- section also Reported sound of horse and motor transport moving towards LA BASSEE about 9 pm AAA Considerable railway activity between 6.30 and 7.15 am this morning in area ROUBAIX ORCHIES DOUAI LENS AAA

FROM
PLACE & TIME

(ROUBAIX)

"C" Form (Duplicate). Army Form C. 2123.
MESSAGES AND SIGNALS. No. of Message:

Charges to Pay. Office Stamp.
£ s. d.
26.III.15

Service Instructions.

Handed in at **ULO** Office **10.55** m. Received **11.0** m.

TO 2nd Cav Div

| Sender's Number | Day of Month | In reply to Number | AAA |

General movement towards LENS and DOUAI

2nd Div C/31
11-10 am

FROM PLACE & TIME 1st Corps 10.43 am

"C" Form (Duplicate). Army Form C. 2123.
MESSAGES AND SIGNALS. No. of Message

Service Instructions.

Handed in at ___ Office ___ m. Received ___ m.

TO 2nd London Divn

Sender's Number	Day of Month	In reply to Number	AAA
G 476	20th		

Two motor busses will be sent out Sunday 28th to take six officers and six ncos to headqrs 2nd Infantry Bde at ESE DV RAUX N of LOISNE and nine officers and nine NCOs to 3rd Infy Bde headqrs at RICHEBOURG ST VAAST AAA Both parties will arrive at destination 3 pm AAA further instructions will be sent later AAA addressed 2nd London Repeated 1st Division

FROM PLACE & TIME 1st Corps 10.20 pm

2nd LONDON DIVISION, T.F.

BILLETING AREAS ON MARCH 27th.

Headquarters Area.

Divl.H.Q., H.Q.R.A., H.Q.& No.1 Scn.Signal Co., Cyclist Coy., H.Q.& H.Q.Co.Train.	MARLES-LEZ-MINES.
H.Q.R.E. and Divl.Ammn.Col.	LOZINGHEM.

4th Brigade Area.

H.Q. 4th Lon.Inf.Bde.	AUCHEL.
* 6th Battn.London Regt.	RAIMBERT.
* 7th ,, ,,	AUCHEL.
* 8th ,, ,,	AUCHEL.
15th ,, ,,	CAUCHY.
4th Lon.Fd.Ambulance.	AUCHEL.
No.2 Company Train.	AUCHEL.
Divl Supply Column.	AUCHEL.
7th Lon.Bde. R.F.A.	AUCHEL.
8th Lon.(How) Bde.R.F.A.	FERFAY.

5th Brigade Area.

H.Q.5th Lon.Inf.Bde.	CHATEAU St.ANDRE' ¼ mile W of MENSECQ.
17th Battn.London Regt.	HURIONVILLE.
18th ,, ,,	BURBURE.
19th ,, ,,	ALLOUAGNE.
20th ,, ,,	ALLOUAGNE.
5th Lon Fd.Ambulance.	ALLOUAGNE.
No.3 Company Train.	BURBURE.
5th Lon.Bde. R.F.A.	ECQUEDECQUES.
2nd Lon.Heavy Batty.& Ammo.Col.	LIERES.

6th Brigade Area.

H.Q. 6th Lon.Inf.Bde.	LABEUVRIERE.
21st Battn.London Regt.	OBLINGHEM.
22nd ,, ,,	VENDIN.
23rd ,, ,,	LABEUVRIERE.
24th ,, ,,	LAPUGNOY.
6th Lon.Fd.Ambulance.	LABEUVRIERE.
No.4 Company Train.	LABEUVRIERE.
6th Lon.Bde. R.F.A.	LAPUGNOY.

* Temporarily detached.

REPORT ON WORK OF 2ND LONDON DIVISION BATTALIONS ATTACHED TO 2ND DIVISION.

8th P.O. Rifles.   1.   3 platoons in 2nd line, and 6 or 7 officers
with 4th Brigade.   sleeping in the trenches.
                             Employed on new communication trenches and
did good work; shells falling near them while employed, and hurting no one.
They have been well taught not to bunch and crowd together.

6th London Regiment.   2.   1 company in the trenches.
with 6th Brigade.   2 companies digging between CUINCHY and PONT FIXE road.
1 company training between ANNEQUIN and BETHUNE.

7th London Regiment.   3.   Two platoons were attached to the Oxford &
with 5th Brigade.   Bucks, L.I., and two to the Worcestershire
Regt for 24 hours. They were put in front line by sections; two reliefs each of 100 men were employed filling sandbags for new breastworks. The battalion Staff were attached to battalions in the front line for instruction.

27th March, 1915.

Major-General.
Commanding 2nd Division.

Hd Quarters
4th London Inf. Bde
For your information, please return.
H.R. Hunt Capt
G.S.
28/3/15

3.

Headquarters - 2nd London Division

Noted and returned -

G. Cuthbert
  Brig. General
Cmd 4th London Infantry Brigade.

29/3/15.
Bm/158.B.

2nd London Division

Instruction of 6th, 7th, & 8th, London battalions.

6th Battalion. (attached to 6th Infy Bde). Second company now doing trench duty. One other company has been digging, one training and one cleaning up after duty in the trenches.

7th Battalion. (attached to 5th Infy Bde) A second company doing trench duty for 24 hours. Remainder training and filling sandbags. Battalion Staff attached to battalions in front line.

8th Battalion. (attached to 4th (Guards) Bde). 3 platoons in trenches for 24 hours. Two companies digging and repairing works. More officers spent the night in the trenches.

28th March 1915.

Louis Vaughan Lt Col
for Major-General.
Commanding 2nd Division.

4th Lon. Inf. Bde

For information & return please

Lt. Colonel
GENERAL STAFF
2nd LONDON DIVISION.

- 3 -

Headquarters,
2nd Lon. Div.

Noted & returned.

G. Cuthbert

2nd London Division

INSTRUCTION OF 6th, 7th & 8th LONDON BATTNS.

for 24 hours ending noon 29th

6th Battalion (attached to 6th Infantry Brigade.)

A third company on trench duty for 24 hours.
One other company digging, one training and one cleaning up after trench duty.

7th Battalion. (attached to 5th Infantry Brigade.)

A third company in trenches, and remainder continuing instruction as yesterday.

8th Battalion. (attached to 4th (Guards) Brigade.)

Three more platoons in trenches for 24 hours, with N.C.O's of Guards Brigade detailed to give them all information.
Two companies employed on various works.

For Information

(sd) H.S. Horne

Major-General,
29th March, 1915.   Commanding 2nd Division.

(2)

2nd London Division

For information

J A Bouzzard Major
f Lt Col G.S.
S.G.S.O
2nd Division

March 29th 1915

4th Lon. Inf. Bde.

For information and return.

[signature]

Lt. Colonel
GENERAL STAFF
2nd LONDON DIVISION.

4.

Headquarters,
2nd London Division.

Noted and returned.

G. Cuthbert
Brigadier General,
Comdg. 4th Lon. Inf. Bde.

BM/198
31st March, 1915.

SUBJECT. Instruction of Territorial Battalions.

2nd London Division.

6th London Battalion. (attached 6th Infy. Brigade.)
      As yesterday.

7th London Battalion. (attached 5th Infy. Brigade.)
      One company took up right of "C"1.
      Two reliefs of 100 men employed, working on breastworks.

8th London Battalion. (attached 4th (Guards) Brigade.)
      All platoons have now had experience in front line, and a complete company will relieve a company in B.3 tonight.

Louis Vaughan

31st March 1915.
                                 Lieut-Colonel.
                              General Staff. 2nd Division.
                              for Maj. General
                              Comdg 2nd Division

G.O.C.
4th London Inf. Bde.

For your information and return, please.

                              Major
                              General Staff
                              2nd London Div.

Head Quarters 2nd Lon: Division

Noted & returned.

G. Cuthbert
Brig: General
Comdg 4th London Inf. Brigade

[Stamp: BRIGADE OFFICE / 1 - APR. 1915 / 4TH LONDON INFANTRY BRIGADE]

"A" Form. Army Form C. 2121.

MESSAGES AND SIGNALS.

TO	1st Corps

Sender's Number	Day of Month	In reply to Number	AAA
C 2 8	Twentyninth	C 467	

Following numbers available aaa officers
thirty five n c os thirty two

From 2nd London Div
Place
Time 8·45 am

"C" Form (Duplicate).　　Army Form C. 2123.
MESSAGES AND SIGNALS.

OHMS 36　A20

Office Stamp: 29.III.15

Handed in at R.O.　Office　m. Received

TO　2nd London Div

Sender's Number	Day of Month	In reply to Number	AAA
G179	29		

AUBERS HERLIES ILLIES SALOME HANTAY BERCLAU DOUVRIN HAISNES clear of formed bodies between 6.30 and 7.50 am aaa addressed first and second repeated second London

2L Div G/49
9.20 am

FROM PLACE & TIME　1st Corps 9.0 am

"A" Form.   Army Form C. 2121.

MESSAGES AND SIGNALS.

TO: ~~GRA~~ Second Lon. Div. Arty

Sender's Number: 1G/56

Please detail 1 Officer and 2 Gunners to proceed to Maison ANDRIEN ~~Quartier~~ Rue du ~~Bac~~ Nord ST VENANT tomorrow 30th inst ~~AAA~~ for instruction in use of trench mortars AAA Care must be taken in the selection of Officer and men who should be volunteers if possible and specially qualified as to physique conduct eyesight &c. for the work. AAA acknowledge.

From: Second Lon Div.
Time: 12.20 pm

Signature: HR Hunt Capt

"A" Form.
MESSAGES AND SIGNALS.
Army Form C. 2121.

TO	4th Inf	5th Bde	6th	Lon

Sender's Number: *1457
Day of Month: Twenty ninth
AAA

Course of instruction in use of small Trench Mortar will start tomorrow 30th inst. AAA Following will attend 4th Lon Inf Bde one private 5th Inf. Bde one officer 6th Inf. Bde one private. These will be volunteers if possible and specially qualified as to physique conduct eyesight &c for the work AAA They will report at MAISON ANDRIEN RUE DU NORD ST tomorrow AAA Acknowledge

From: Second Lon. Div.
Place:
Time: 12.40 p.m.

(Z) H.R. Hunt Capt G.S.

"A" Form. Army Form C. 2121.
MESSAGES AND SIGNALS. No. of Message_____

| Prefix____ Code____ m. | Words. | Charge. | This message is on a/c of: | Recd. at____ m. |
| Office of Origin and Service Instructions. | Sent At____ m. To____ By____ | | _____Service. (Signature of "Franking Officer.") | Date____ From____ By____ |

TO { 1st Corps

| Sender's Number | Day of Month | In reply to Number | AAA |
| G 60 | 29 | 265 G | |

are SAA sections of Brig
Amm Cols to move aaa this
also applies to SAA in Div
Amm Col which it is understood
is also about to be ordered to
move

From 2nd London Div
Place
Time 6.40 pm

The above may be forwarded as now corrected. (Z) _____ Whitchurch
Censor. Major
Signature of Addresser or person authorised to telegraph in his name
* This line should be erased if not required.
(24473). M.R.Co., Ltd. Wt. W4843/541. 50,000. 9/14. Forms C2121/10.

SECRET.

~~2nd Division.~~

2nd London Division.
───────────

The move of the Divisional Artillery 2nd London Division into 2nd Division area will be carried out as follows :-

1. March 30th, 3 p.m.- Brigade and battery commanders report at Headquarters 2nd Divisional Artillery for attachment to brigades. These officers will be provided with billets and must be prepared to remain for ten days or a fortnight. They must make their own arrangements for messing.

2. They will reconnoitre the positions for their batteries and study the German position from their observation stations.

3. They will come under the orders of the commanders of the brigades to which they are attached as follows :-

X 20 d.	5th London Brigade. 1 battery 6th London Bde. 1 " 7th " "	To 36th Brigade, R.F.A. at LE HAMEL.
A 26.	6th London Brigade, less 1 battery.	To 41st Brigade, R.F.A. at CAMBRIN.
F 10 b.	7th London Brigade, less 1 battery.	To 34th Brigade, R.F.A. at canal junction LE PREOL.
F 8	5" Howitzer Brigade, less 1 battery.	To 44th Brigade, R.F.A. at LE QUESNOY.

4. April 2nd, evening.- 5" Howitzer Battery moves to position and registers on 3rd.

5. April 3rd.- 15 pr. brigades move into positions and register on 4th and 5th.

3-45 p.m.
29th March, 1915.

Rubingham Brig. General.
S.G.S.O., 1st Corps.

"A" Form.   Army Form C. 2121.

MESSAGES AND SIGNALS.

TO: 2nd London Div: Eng:

Sender's Number: G 62
Day of Month: 30

Staves and Brushwood are required by all battns: for training in revetment etc aaa Supply is to be through R E Park aaa Arrange for suitable quantities and inform me of exact place from which the above must be fetched in order that transport may be arranged

From: 2nd London Div
Time: 7.52 a.m.

"C" Form (Duplicate).   Army Form C. 2123.
MESSAGES AND SIGNALS.   No. of Message

Charges to Pay. — Office Stamp: YL 30.III.15 B

Service Instructions.

Handed in at the aco Office, at 10.35 a.m. Received here at 10.3_ a.m.

TO: 2nd London Div

Sender's Number.	Day of Month.	In reply to Number.	AAA
L.G.181	30		

Air reconnaissance 7.10 a.m AAA no unusual movement in front of first Corps front AAA addressed first and second Divs repeated Second London

2 L.D. 4/59
Recd 10.19 a.m

FROM: 1st Corps
PLACE:
TIME: 10 AM

"C" Form (Duplicate).
MESSAGES AND SIGNALS.
Army Form C. 2123.
No. of Message.

Charges to Pay. £ s. d.

Office Stamp.

Service Instructions.

Handed in at ACO Office m. Received m.

TO 2nd LONDON DIV

Sender's Number	Day of Month	In reply to Number	AAA
G 503	30		

Paras 4 and 5 of first Corps memorandum G 265 (9) issued at 3.45 pm 29th March are cancelled AAA instructions will be issued later regarding the move of these batteries AAA added 2nd ACo 2nd LON Div

2 Div G/60
3.55/pm

FROM PLACE & TIME 1st CORPS 3.20

"A" Form. Army Form C. 2121.

MESSAGES AND SIGNALS.

TO: Second Lon Div Arty

Sender's Number	Day of Month	In reply to Number	AAA
I.G/65	Thirty		

Paras Four and Five Of 1st Corps memo 265 G issued at 3-45 pm 29th March are cancelled aaa Instructions will be issued later regarding the move of these Batteries aaa Acknowledge.

From: Second Lon Div.
Place:
Time: 4-15 pm

"C" Form (Duplicate). Army Form C. 2123.

MESSAGES AND SIGNALS. No. of Message.

From BH? 37

Service Instructions.

Handed in at ___ Office ___ m. Received ___ m.

TO 2nd LONDON DIV

Sender's Number	Day of Month	In reply to Number	AAA
Y502	30		

In view of changed situation battery 8th London Bde will not be sent tomorrow added 2nd Corps and 2nd London Div

Copy sent to 2 Div 9/61
See Arty 4.15 pm
See for W.D. 13th by Q Branch

FROM PLACE & TIME 1st CORPS 2.20pm

"A" Form.　　Army Form C. 2121
MESSAGES AND SIGNALS.

TO: Second Lon Div Arty

Sender's Number: G.66
Day of Month: 30
AAA

The following message received from 1st Corps begins AAA G502 March 30th AAA In view of changed situation battery 8th London Bde will not be sent to-morrow addsd 1nd corps and 2nd London Div ends. Acknowledge

From: Second Lon Div
Time: 4-15 pm

"A" Form.　　　　　　　　　　　　　　　Army Form C. 2121.
MESSAGES AND SIGNALS.　　No. of Message _____

PRIORITY

TO { 1st Corps

Sender's Number	Day of Month	In reply to Number	AAA
G-69	Thirtieth	C-502	

Your wire orders move of battery 8th
London Brig NOT to be sent tomorrow - aaa
presume this cancels your 257 G dated
25th March which ordered a battery
of this Brig to join MEERUT DIV on
3rd April

From 2nd London Div
Place
Time 6.27 pm

MESSAGES AND SIGNALS.

Army Form C. 2121.

"A" Form.

TO: Second Lon Div Arty
Fourth Lon Inf Bde
Fifth Lon Inf Bde
Sixth Lon Inf Bde.

Sender's Number: G/70 Shurketh

AAA

The issue of Brassards to interpreters will take place as notified in Routine Orders No 11 para one of today which was cancelled in copies issued AAA Please instruct interpreters in your area accordingly AAA

From: Second Lon Div.
Time: 6.55 pm.

R. Hunt Capt G.S.

"C" Form (Duplicate).   Army Form C. 2123.
MESSAGES AND SIGNALS.   No. of Message.

Service Instructions.

Handed in at _____ Office _____ m. Received _____ m.

TO 2nd LONDON DIVN

Sender's Number	Day of Month	In reply to Number	AAA
G306	30th	9/69	

Move of 5th Howitzer Battery
8th London Bde will be
postponed till further orders

2L Div 9/62
7-25 pm

FROM PLACE & TIME: 1st CORPS 7.10 pm

MESSAGES AND SIGNALS. Army Form C. 2121.

TO: 4th London Inf Bde / 5th " " " / 6th " " ") alt) Cyclist Coy (except last sentence)

Sender's Number: C 67 Day of Month: Thirtieth AAA

Officers selected for training as bomb and grenadier officers will attend at 78 RUE DE LILLE BETHUNE on the BETHUNE – LA BASSEE road at 3pm on 1st April when the O.C. Bomb factory will give them an exhibition aaa It is essential that officers be punctual aaa They will find their way under Bnjock arrangements as regards transport

From: 2nd London Div
Time: 5.15 am

"C" Form (Duplicate).   Army Form C. 2123.

MESSAGES AND SIGNALS.   No. of Message

SM SDR 36 am aro na

Charges to Pay. £ s. d.

Office Stamp. YL 31.III.15

Service Instructions.

Handed in at .... Office 9.21 am. Received 9.27 am.

TO: 2nd LONDON DIV

Sender's Number	Day of Month	In reply to Number	AAA
AG 183	31		

Air reconnaissance 6.15 to 7.35 am AAA No unusual movement behind German lines on first Corps front AAA addressed First and Second Divs repeated Second London

2 L.D. G/64
Recd 9.35 am

FROM PLACE & TIME: 1st CORPS 9.20 am

Wt. W1154/2246. 7/11. 7,500,000. Sch. 4a. "A" Form. Army Form C. 2121.

MESSAGES AND SIGNALS.

No. of Message _____

Prefix	Code	m.	Words	Charge	This message is on a/c of.	Recd. at _____ m.
Office of Origin and Service Instructions.			Sent		_____ Service.	Date _____
			At _____ m.			From _____
			To _____			
			By _____		(Signature of "Franking Officer.")	By _____

TO { 2ⁿᵈ Division

| Sender's Number. | Day of Month | In reply to Number | |
| G 74 | Thirtyfirst | | A A A |

Can you say on what date the next
three battalions for training can be
received aaa The battalions will be
15ᵗʰ 17ᵗʰ and 18ᵗʰ London Regt

From 2ⁿᵈ London Div
Place
Time 3 pm

The above may be forwarded as now corrected.   (Z) Monnett Walthorth
                                                    Major
Censor. Signature of Addresser or person authorised to telegraph in his name.

* This line should be erased if not required.

"C" Form (Duplicate).   Army Form C. 2123.

MESSAGES AND SIGNALS.   No. of Message

		Charges to Pay.	Office Stamp.
Tom G.B.S. 38	aco	£ s. d.	YL 31.10.15 TELEGRAPHS
	CR		

Service Instructions.

Handed in at ACO   Office 5-12 p.m.   Received 5-17 p.m.

TO   2nd LONDON DIV

Sender's Number	Day of Month	In reply to Number	AAA
G 511	31		

Following message received from Second Army begins Germans are now sending out air reconnaissance at about three am ends addressed 1st Div 2nd Div repeated 2nd London Div

2 Lon. Div / 65 / C

5.20 pm

FROM PLACE & TIME   1st Corps   5.12 pm

MESSAGES AND SIGNALS.

Army Form C.2123.

No. of Message _____

Charges to Pay: £ s. d.

Office Stamp.

Service Instructions. Blandford

Handed in at 2nd Divn. Office 7.16 p.m. Received 7.50 p.m.

TO: 2nd London Divn

Sender's Number	Day of Month	In reply to Number	AAA
G488	31	G74	

The three battn now with this divn will leave Bethune to rejoin you on morning of 7th inst HJH three battns to replace them will probably be ordered to arrive in Bethune on evening of 7th inst but nothing definite can be said until orders are received from 1st Corps

21.0 G/66
7.55 p.m.

FROM PLACE & TIME: 2nd Divn 7.15 pm

MESSAGES AND SIGNALS.

Army Form C. 2121.

TO Second Division

Sender's Number: 475
Day of Month: Thirty first
AAA

May Brigadier General Commanding 5th London Infantry Brigade with his staff be attached for a few days from Monday 5th instant and G.O.C. 6th London Infantry Brigade from Thursday 8th inst with staff AAA They understand that they must arrange for billets and mess in BETHUNE as was done by 5th London Infantry Brigade

From Second London Divn.
Time 8/47 p.m.

H.R. Hunt Capt

"C" Form (Duplicate). Army Form C. 2123.

MESSAGES AND SIGNALS.

| Handed in at ACO | Office 10.35 | Received 11.0 |

TO 2nd LONDON DIV

Sender's Number	Day of Month	In reply to Number	AAA
G 515	31		

Please wire by 8 am tomorrow which Battalions have been selected to go to 1st Army on 2nd April AAA They should be warned that they will probably have to march tomorrow afternoon

2 Lon Div/68/G
11.0 pm

FROM PLACE & TIME 1st CORPS 10.45 pm

15th & 17th isn't it?
Will write message & warn
Belle tonight in case 17th
are for range.
                    JRH.

Hitchcock says
15th 2 Bn of 4th Inf Belle
        and
17th Bn of 5 L Inf Bd
    @
            HVD

"A" Form. Army Form C. 2121.
MESSAGES AND SIGNALS.

TO: 1st Corps

Sender's Number: 1G 77
Day of Month: thirty-first
In reply to Number: G 515
AAA

15th and 17th Battalion London Regt selected to go to 1st Division on 2nd April

Cancelled

From: Second Echelon, AW
Time: 11.37 p.m.

AR Hunt Capt G.S.

"A" Form.   Army Form C. 2121.
MESSAGES AND SIGNALS.   No. of Message_____

Prefix____ Code____ m. | Words. | Charge. | This message is on a/c of: | Recd. at____ m.
Office of Origin and Service Instructions. | Sent At____ m. To____ By____ | | ____Service. (Signature of "Franking Officer.") | Date____ From____ By____

TO { FOURTH LON INF BDE
     FIFTH LON INF BDE

| Sender's Number | Day of Month | In reply to Number | A A A |
| * 1G78 Hungerford | | | |

15th and 17th Battalions London Regt
selected to go to 1st Division on 2nd April
warn Battalions that they will probably
have to march afternoon tomorrow 1st
April AAA Acknowledge

Cancelled

From Second Lon Div
Place
Time 11.37 pm.
The above may be forwarded as now corrected. (Z)

BM/177

INFANTRY LINE OF 6TH, 7TH, 8TH, LONDON BATTALIONS.

8th London Battalion.

Work as yesterday.

7th London Battalion.

Work as yesterday.

Tonight they commence holding a portion of the line as one complete company.

8th London Battalion.

2 companies, and 3 platoons usefully employed.

Louis Vaughan Lt Col
for Major-General.
Commanding 2nd Division.

29th March 1915.

4th Lon.Inf.Bde.

For information and return.

Lt.Colonel
GENERAL STAFF
2nd LONDON DIVISION.

P.T.O.

3

Head Quarters 2nd Lon Div.

Noted & returned.

G. Cuthbert

Brig: General
Comdg 4th London Inf. Brigade

MESSAGES AND SIGNALS.

TO: 2 Lon Div

Sender's Number: G.515
Day of Month: 31
AAA

Please wire by 8 am tomorrow which Battn have been selected to go to 1st Div on 2nd April aau they should be warned that they will probably have to march tomorrow afternoon.

2D S/68
11-0 pm

From: 1st Corps
Time: 10-45 pm

War Diary

47th Div.

General Staff

April 1915

On His Majesty's Service.

81st Brigade.

Appendices to War Diary. Vol. IV.

WAR DIARY

Army Form C. 398.

To:— *Ludendorff
War Diary (C.S.)
Attached
1st April*

DESPATCH.	RECEIPT.
Sender's No.	Date .... hour .... m.
Date .... hour .... m.	Signature:—

URGENT or ORDINARY.

2nd LONDON DIVISION, T.F.
****

WAR DIARY (GENERAL STAFF).

APRIL, 1915.
****

MARLES LES MINES.   1st April 1915.

    Frost again at night.   Very fine day; clear, little wind.

7-35 a.m.   S.C. from 1st Corps arrived and explained that there were no billets available for marching up our battns from South for attachment to 1st Division.   Overnight detail was therefore cancelled and 21st and 22nd Battns.of 6th Lon.Inf.Bde. now at OBLINGHEM and VENDIN (near BETHUNE) detailed for attachment 2nd, and warned might move on 1st. 1st Corps also informed of fresh detail.   G/79,80,81.

    Instructions received as to deceiving the enemy as to future operations -
    (a). Shelters for troops in rear of 1st Line.
    (b). Fire opened whenever enemy shows activity.
    (c). Registration at daybreak.   Secret 1st Corps 274 (G).
    (d). Occasional removal of our own wire.   G/57.

    Operations to take place on 3rd April. 1st Corps and Indian Corps.   Secret 1st Corps 267 (G).
    G/58.

3-30 p.m.   Orders received for 2 battalions 6th Lon.Inf.Bde. to join 1st Division for attachment 8 - 12 days tomorrow. Brigade and A & Q informed.   Wired 1st Division for destination and time of arrival desired, and asked if   G/2/6. Brigade Staff could be accommodated for a few days.   G/85.
    1st Corps 251 (G).

4-15 p.m.   G.O.C. 1st Corps inspected Divl.Ammn. Column (less Heavy portion).

5-0 p.m.   Br.Gen. G.S. 1st Corps lectured C.O's and Adjts on Attack in Trench Warfare exemplified by NEUVE CHAPELLE.

6-5 p.m.   Instructions from 1st Division for attachment of battalions tomorrow.
22nd Battn. to 3rd Inf.Bde. at RICHEBOURG ST VAAST. 1st Div. 238 (G).
21st Battn. to 1st (Guards) Bde. at LE TOURET (X 17 c).   G/86.
Further notification will be sent re Brigade Staff   G/91.
6th Lon.Inf.Bde.   A & Q informed.

8-35 p.m.   6th Lon.Inf.Bde. to be attached to 3rd Inf.Bde.   G/92.
from tomorrow.   1st Div. 540 (G).

MARLES LES MINES.   2nd April 1915.

    No frost. Bright sun - little wind - slight rain after 8 p.m.

    Further instructions received as to rendering   G/51/2.
reports when in first line - filed G.S.O.(3).   1st Corps 266 (G).

    Heavy portion Div.Ammn.Col. returned to LOZINGHEM last night from MEERUT Divn. apparently an error as they were called back this morning; question taken up.

R.A. Officers attached to 2nd Divn. to rejoin their units.   G/521. 1st C.
G/503. 2nd D.

Aeroplanes not to be fired on between 3 and 7 a.m. tomorrow   Secret   G/280. 1st C.
No.66/G.
Circulated . G/101.

All passages of hostile aeroplanes westward to be reported by telegram to 1st Corps. Circulated .   G/277. 1st C.
G/64.

3 battns of 4th Lon.Inf.Bde. now attached to 2nd Divn. return morning of 7th instant and are replaced in evening one 4th Bde. and two 5th Bde. .   G/98 & 99.

MARLES LES MINES.   3rd April, 1915.

Slight rain during night. Dull morning. Wet day after 9 a.m.

Instructions received as to communication with the enemy, varying those previously issued. .   G/1089. 1st C.
Circulated Confidential . G/69.

General Vesey Dawson, Inspector of Infantry, inspects 5th Lon.Inf.Bde. at 2-45 p.m. .   G/108.

Informed 1st Corps of position of Inf.Bde.H.Qrs. 4th - AUCHEL, 5th - MENSECQ, 6th - tempy RICHEBOURG ST VAAST attached to 3rd Inf.Bde. normally LABEUVRIERE.   G/530. 1st C.
G/109.

Moves on 7th :-
15th Bn. to ECOLE DE JEUNES FILLES   .   Attd. 4th Bde.
17th Bn. to MONTMORENCY Barracks, BETHUNE ,, 5th Bde.   G/531. 2nd D.
18th Bn. to ORPHANAGE.   .   ,, 6th Bde.   I.G/110.
Billeting parties report 11 a.m. Battalions to arrive after 3 p.m.

Return of 6th, 7th, and 8th Bns on 7th. .   G/541. 2nd D.
G.T/115.

1-8 p.m.   Air report 5-45 - 6-45 a.m. No movement HAISNES - AUCHY - LORGIES.   I.G/185. 1st C.

4-0 p.m.   5th Lon.Inf.Bde. report wire tapping and orderlies assaulted last night. They are taking steps. O.C.Signal Coy, and A.P.M. informed. Probably nonsense. S.C/281. 5th B.

10-11 p.m.   Attachment of officers and N.C.O's to 1st Divn to cease now that they have taken two battalions.   G/535. 1st C.

MARLES LES MINES.   Easter Sunday. 4th April 1915.

Dull misty morning. Slight rain at intervals until 4 p.m.

H.Q. 5th Lon.Inf.Bde. to billet in BETHUNE and arrange with Inf.Bdes. of 2nd Div. to see the work.

3.

5th April, 1915.

MARLES LES MINES.
    Wet night, misty, wet all day, heavy rain in afternoon.
    G.S.O's 1 and 2 visited FESTUBERT Section of 2nd Division line.

MARLES LES MINES.   6th April 1915.

    Rain stopped during night. Bright clear morn; clouded over at noon. Rain 3 p.m.
    G.S.O.2 visited NEUVE CHAPELLE Secn; left of 1st Division.

In accordance with telephone message from 1st Corps asked 1st Div. if 22nd Bn.returns (from 3rd Inf.Bde.) on 8th, and 21st Bn.(from 1st Bde) on 11th. 1st Div.replied that this was correct. 23rd Bn.to rejoin 1st Bde. on 11th; Coys at LE TOURET at 6 p.m. H.Qrs & Transport billet in X 14 c during afternoon. A.&.Q. informed re supplies and 6th Lon.Inf.Bde.informed.	G/577/1st D. G.H/122,123, 125, 127, 131.
No.11 Anti-aircraft Secn. moved to X 27 a N.	G/550/1st C.
10-20 p.m. Telephone from 1st Corps (Maj.H.Wake) 5 battns instead of 3 to be attached to 2nd Divn. from tomorrow. Vendin billets to be given up to 2nd Div. Proposal is to complete training of our infantry by 16th instant. Warned remaining 2 bns of 5th Lon.Inf.Bde. to march to BETHUNE tomorrow afternoon. Information A.&.Q. re VENDIN Billets.	G/557/1st C.
19th Lon.Bn.attached to 5th Bde. 20th Bn.attached to 6th Bde. Billets BETHUNE.	G.H/132. G.H/133.

MARLES LES MINES.   7th April 1915.

    Rain most of night. Fine morning. More wind. Showers during afternoon.

7-30 a.m. Received information of Squadron King Edwards Horse being en route to join Division. Secret.	G/142/1st C. G/75.
Received No.6 copy of proposals for action by G.O.C. 1st Corps to 1st Army. Secret.	G/289/1st C. G/76.
10-0 a.m. Conference at Div.Arty.H.Q. 15 pdr. and 5" Howr. Bdes. to be put in as soon as possible for training. Gunners go up tomorrow to dig emplacements, guns on Saturday. Ammunition allow 3 rds per gun per diem.	G/265/1st C. G/80. 1966/7/1st C. G/79.Secret to Div.Arty.
8-18 p.m. Artillery movement above postponed for 24 hours. Divisional Artillery informed.	G/597/2nd D. G.H/143 & 4.
10-2 p.m. 4th Lon.Fd.Co.R.E. to return from 2nd Div.tomorrow. C.R.E. to arrange move and report.	G/569/1st C. G.B/145.

MARLES LES MINES.   8th April 1915.

    Very little rain at night. Fine colder morning. Cold storms at intervals.

    Situation night 8th/9th April :-

Div.H.Q., Cyclist Coy.,Mobile Vet. Secn. and Train.	MARLES LES MINES.
H.Q.Div.Engrs., Div.Ammn.Column.	LOZINGHEM.
4th Fd.Co.R.E. & 5th Lon.Fd.Amb.	ALLOUAGNE.From attd.2nd Div.(25/3).
3rd ,,	BURBURE. From 28th Divn.

4.

H.Q.Div.Arty.	LOZINGHEM, to BETHUNE 9th.
5th Lon.F.A.Brigade.	ECQUEDECQUES.)
6th "	LAPUGNOY.) To 2nd Div.11th.
7th "	AUCHEL.)
8th "	FERFAY. To)1st Div. 11th.
2nd London Heavy Battery.	Detached to No.1 Group Heavy Reserve Artillery - VIEILLE - CHAPELLE.
H.Q.4th L.Inf.Bde.,4th L.Fd.Amb.	AUCHEL.)
7th & 8th Lon.Battalions.	AUCHEL.) Attached 2nd Div. (24/3 -
6th "	RAIMBERT.) - 7/4).
15th "	BETHUNE. Attd.4th Inf.Bde.(7th).
H.Q. 5th Lon.Inf.Bde.	MENSECQ. To BETHUNE on 10th.
17th and 19th Lon.Battalions.	BETHUNE Attd.5th Inf.Bde. (7th).
18th and 20th "	BETHUNE Attd.6th Inf.Bde. (7th).
H.Q.6th Lon.Inf.Bde.,6th L.F.Amb.	LABEUVRIERE.
21st London Battalion.	Attd.1st Inf.Bde.(1st).To LAPUGNOY 11th.
22nd "	LABEUVRIERE. From Attd.3rd Inf.Bde.
23rd "	OBLINGHEM. To 1st Inf.Bde. (11th).
24th "	LAPUGNOY.
Divl.Supply Column.	AUCHEL.

4-0 p.m.   1st Corps Operation Order No. 76 received. Secret. No. 76/2.
                                                                G.B/154.

6-15 p.m. G.O.C. held conference for officers and N.C.O's
    of 6th Lon.Bn. on the subject of Attack from Trenches.

MARLES LES MINES.   9th April, 1915.

    Received Secret Instructions for showing artillery   G/297/1st C.
    objectives on maps.   G/86.
        Secret - Duties of Arty.Advisers defined.   G/292/1st C.
    Copies of both to Divl.Arty.   G/87.
        Fine dry night, dull morning, storms at intervals.
        Successors to command Divn.,Div.Arty. and Inf.Bdes.
    nominated.   Secret . G/89.

7-10 p.m. Air report. All clear to our front.   .   . I.G/192/1st C.

MARLES LES MINES.   10th April 1915.

    Some rain during night. Fine day; bright at intervals.

    5th Lon.Inf.Bde.H.Q. moved to 77 Boulevard Victor Hugo,
        BETHUNE.
        Instructions for use of one round Lyddite per gun   1966/7/1st C.
    per diem for 5" Howrs. Forwarded to Div.Arty. Secret.   G/79/2.

    C.R.A. - 15 Place de la Republique, BETHUNE.

        G.O.C. visited trenches of 4th Inf.Bde.

        G.S.O's 1 and 2 visited gun emplacements being
    prepared by Div.Arty. 8th Bde.(How) with 1st Divn.
    15 pdr.Bdes.(2 batteries in action and 1 in reserve per
    Bde) with 2nd Division.

        Memo - Precautions against espoinage recd.Confl.   G/191.1st C.
                                                G.S.O.3.   G/90.

7-32.p.m. Air report. No unusual movements.   .   I.G/194/1st C.

MARLES LES MINES.   Sunday 11th April 1915.

    Slight frost at night. Bright, still, sunny morning.

    Report of 2 Arty.Offrs.visiting Sussex Regt. lines (1st Divn); supposed to be spies. In accordance with telephone instructions from 1st Corps, repeated to Div.Arty. to enquire if any of his officers were looking for Observation Stations in NEUVE CHAPELLE. These turned out to be offrs of 7th Divn.   .   .   .   .

G/597. 1st C.

G.B.160.

P.121. 1st C.

    Tracing showing positions of batteries, observing stations, and centre of zones of fire of 15 pdr.batteries in action - received.

6-55 p.m. Report of German Taube passing over LABEUVRIERE at 5-50 p.m.   .   .   .

B.M/344.

    Only two batteries per F.A.Bde. go into action. Other batteries remain in present billets. Relief to take place within F.A.B. for training purposes.

MARLES LES MINES.   12th April 1915.

    Fine night. Cloudy morning. Colder day - no rain.

    G.O.C. inspected 1st Line Transport of 4th Lon. Inf.Bde. and of 6th, 7th, & 8th Battns; of 4th and 5th Lon.Fd.Ambces; 3rd and 4th Fd.Cos., and also Divl.Ammn.Column.

    Divl.Ammunition Column moved to ANNEZIN.

11-40 a.m. Air report 9-30 a.m. Roads to our front clear of movement. Railway trains normal. Large quantity of timber in LA BASSEE.

G/612. 1st C.

    Instructions for officers visiting areas held by other Divisions to report at Div.H.Q. concerned for authority. Received and circulated.

    Late evening air reconnaissances are now being undertaken by both sides.

MARLES LES MINES.   13th April 1915.

    Fine night. Foggy morning. Dull day.

7-10 a.m. Airship passed over BAILLEUL (3rd Corps), dropping bombs, coming from S.E. at 11-3 p.m.

G/619. 1st C.

    Wastage of Division to date - one month in France - all ranks.
10 killed, 75 wounded, and 62 sick evacuated.

    G.O.C.inspected 1st Line Tpt. of 21st, 23rd, and 24th Bns. (6th Lon.Inf.Bde); 6th Lon.Fd.Amb.;

    Received Artillery Ammunition Distribution. Secret. To D.A. to note and return.   .   .

G/79/3.

    Notes on Co-op - Aircraft with other arms. Confl.

D.A.2/29.A.
G/8/1.

Suspicious officer asking questions of 2nd Divn.	G/624. 1st C.
Description and orders to detain and report.	G/681. 2nd Div.
Circulated. Apprehended elsewhere.	G.B.170 & 171.

        Received 5 copies (13-17) of instructions (continuation) for Operations, with paper A & B attached.   G.575a.1st Army. / G/289. 1st C. / G/76/3.

Distribution - Copy No.13.   G.O.C.Divn.
              ,,   14.   Divl.Arty.
              ,,   15.   4th Lon.Inf.Bde. Communicated to C.R.E.
              ,,   16.   5th   ,,
              ,,   17.   6th   ,,

        G.O.C. 1st Army inspected 4th and 6th Lon.Inf. Bdes., less battns in trenches.

        Reports on Artillery Registration satisfactory on all points.

MARLES LES MINES.   <u>14th April 1915</u>.

        Misty rain during early hours of morning, and at intervals all day.

        Changes in situation -
          H.Q.4th L.Inf.Bde., and
            7th & 8th battalions,   to   ALLOUAGNE.
            6th battalion   .   to   BURBURE.
            3rd & 4th Fd.Cos.R.E.   to   LOZINGHEM.

        Orders received to evacuate AUCHEL and MARLES LES MINES by 17th.   "A and Q".

MARLES LES MINES.   <u>15th April 1915</u>.

        Foggy morning, clearing at 9 a.m. Very fine day.

        G.O.C. held conference with officers and Sergts of 6th Lon.Inf.Bde.H.Qrs., 21st, 22nd, and 24th battalions.

12-10 p.m.	British aircraft flying in vicinity of AIRE up to 8-30 p.m. now. . Circulated .	G/643.1st C. G.H.182.
1-32 p.m.	Air report. 11-15 a.m. No movement.	G/644.1st C.
10 p.m.	15th, 17th, 18th, 19th, and 20th Battalions have completed attachment. Return 17th.	G/703.1st C.

MARLES LES MINES.   <u>16th April, 1915</u>.

    Very fine all day.

        G.O.C. inspected Divisional Cyclist Company.

        Instructions received that Lon.Inf.Bdes. will be affiliated for further training commencing on 19th. 4th Lon.Inf.Bde. to 4th and 6th Inf.Bdes.   G/251/1st C.
          5th   ,,   to 5th Inf.Bde.   G/97.
          6th   ,,   to 3rd Inf.Bde.1st Div.

MARLES LES MINES.   17th April, 1915.

 Slight rain during night. Colder fine day.

11 a.m. Headquarters moved to CHATEAU at MENSECQ ½ mile
of LILLERS. . . . G.B/195.

 Cyclist Company moved to HURIONVILLE.

 Train moved to ECQUEDECQUES.

 Secret
 1st Corps preliminary Operation Order received. 289/G. 1st C.

 Railheads are as heretofore - Supply - CHOCQUES;
Ammunition, ST.VENANT. . Q.

 Anti-aircraft sections - revised distribution. G/99.
 Secret. 164/G. 1st C.
Affiliation of battalions :-

 (6th & 7th Lon.Bns. to 6th Inf.Bde. 6th to BETHUNE on 18th,) A
 (to trenches on 19th.) Sec.
4th L.Inf.Bde(7th to BETHUNE on 19th.)
 (8th & 15th Lon.Bns.to 4th Inf.Bde.15th to trenches on 19th) B
 (8th to LE PREOL on 19th)Sec.

5th L.Inf.Bde(17th,18th,19th & 20th
   Lon.Bns.to 5th Inf.Bde.17th to trenches on 19th)
      18th to GORRE on 19th) C
      19th to LABEUVRIERE 19th)Sec.
      20th to LAPUGNOY on 19th)
      G/97/2.

6th L.Inf.Bde(21st & 24th Lon.Bns.to 3rd I.Bde. to front line on 19th)
   (22nd & 23rd ,, ,, to ALLOUAGNE on 19th)
     B.M./366/6th L.I.Bde.

 20th Battery relieve 19th battery; 17th battery relieve 15th;
in action with 2nd Division night of 17th/18th. B.M/401/D.A.

 G.O.C. held conference with H.Q. 4th Lon.Inf.Bde.;
7th and 8th Battalions.

MENSECQ. Sunday, 18th April, 1915.

 Slight frost, bright sunny morning.

 12th Battery relieves 14th Battery in action today. B.M/437/D.A.

8-47 a.m. Air report - all clear to our front. . G/683/1st C.

 Trench mortar battery to be raised and organised
by infantry officer who has gone through course. Will
be temporarily attached to Cyclist Company.

 Received 1st Corps 289/G - Secret - Draft order
for operations in substitution of instructions dated
17th, which were burnt in accordance with orders. G/76/5.

 Received Order of Battle - Secret. Copy No.74. 235/G/1st C.

MENSECQ.   19th April, 1915.

Slight frost; bright, fine day.

Reporting enemy aeroplanes. Brigades will
report direct to 3rd Squadron R.F.C., repeating to
Divl.H.Q.   Divisions then inform 1st Corps who   277/G/1st C.
inform 1st Wing.   Circulated.   G/64/1.

6th Lon.Inf.Bde.H.Q. moved to LESCLAUMES,X.15.c,
                          at 1 p.m.   B.M/368/6th I.B
4th   ,,   ,,   to 49 Rue du Faubourg,
                     ST.PRY, at 12-30 p.m.

G.O.C. 4th Lon.Inf.Bde. to command GIVENCHY section
20th - 24th April during absence on leave of
G.O.C. 4th Inf.Bde.   Section remains under
2nd Division.

Chateau PHILOMEL, MENSECQ.   20th April, 1915.

Fine night. Dull morning until midday when sun came
through.

Notified that "C" Squadron, King Edwards
Horse leaves England today for Divisional Mounted
Troops.   G/75/2.

G.O.C. and G.S.O. 1 attended 1st Corps
Conference at 10 a.m.   Arranged to move Hd.Qrs.
to BETHUNE by 23rd and to take over a portion of
first line trenches night 24th/25th.

12-45 p.m.   4th Lon.Inf.Bde. move to Hd.Qrs.4th Bde.,
       F.10.b, at 5 p.m.   B.M.628/4th I.B

Designation of Division for communications
in the field altered to "London Division".

G.O.C. 5th Lon.Inf.Bde. to command FESTUBERT   G/781/2nd Div.
Section from tomorrow.   G/H.231.

8-55 p.m.   Air report - normal.   G/712/1st C.

9-30 p.m.   Received 1st Corps instructions 289/G,20/4/15.G/76/6.)
                    ,,   ,,   Op.Order No. 77.   ,, G/76/7.) Secret
                    ,,   ,,   Memo re Hd.Qrs.44th F.A.B.
                                   to 1st Divn. 289/G 20/4/15.G/76/8.)

G.O.C. held Conference 5th Lon.Inf.Bde.H.Q.,
17th & 20th battalions - Trench Warfare.

MENSECQ.   21st April, 1915.

       Slight rain during night. Wet until 9 a.m. Dull.

       G.O.C., G.S.O's 1 and 2, visited trenches about CHOCOLAT MENIER CORNER - FESTUBERT.

       Conference with 2nd Division re taking over on 24th/25th.

SECRET.
Received.	Area maps. 25th April and Concentration for Attack from 1st Corps. To "A & Q".	G/289/1st C. G/76/9.
,,	Economy of Artillery Ammunition; G.H.Q. letter. To Div.Arty.	G/243/1st C. G/79/5.
,,	Mining to cease between midnight and 12-30 a.m. To Div.Engrs.	G/314/1st C. G/39/2.

       Conference with Brigadiers and Heads of Services re taking over on 24th/25th.

       G.O.C. saw 1st Corps Commander re use of RUE DU BOIS which may be used for all traffic.

MENSECQ.   22nd April, 1915.

       Frost. Dull morning. Fine afternoon.

       G.S.O. 2 attended experiment with life saving apparatus, rocket, for throwing telephone line forward.
       Range attained - 220 yards only.

       G.O.C. visited CUINCHY Section with G.S.O.3.

       Day spent

22nd April (contd)

Day spent by all Staff in interviewing Corps and 2nd Division reference our taking over. Considerable difficulty met with owing to 2nd Divn. (A & Q) desiring to retain BETHUNE billets and accommodation, but this was gradually overcome. Move of Divisional Hd.Qrs. consequently postponed from tomorrow.

1st Div.Operation Order No.79, and 2nd Divn. Operation Order No.35, received. Secret. G/76.

We are to take over from 10 a.m. 25th April trench line CUINCHY - CHOCOLAT MENIER CORNER with 4th (Guards) Brigade (CUINCHY & GIVENCHY), 5th Lon. Inf.Bde. (FESTUBERT), 6th Lon.Inf.Bde. (INDIAN VILLAGE - CHOCOLAT MENIER CORNER). 4th (Gds) Brigade, 1st East Anglian Fd.Co.R.E. and 4th Field Ambulance come under our orders, and 4th Lon.Inf. with 4th Lon.Field Ambulance, transferred to 2nd Division. Our Artillery (less Heavy Battery and Howitzers) together with 26th (H) Battery, 34th Bde.R.F.A. and 56th Howr.Battery (less 1 Section) and also 36th Brigade R.F.A. (tempy only), come under our orders. We may call on 47th Battery (Howr) in case of emergency.

5th Lon.Bde.R.F.A. will later pass to control of 1st Division as also 36th Brigade R.F.A. to 2nd Division.

MENSECQ.
23rd April, 1915.

Frost, Bright cold morning - cold wind.

G.S.O.1. came over reference a few details of our taking over, and arranged for us to have MICHELET SCHOOLS ~~Fiel~~ for Field Ambulance on 26th dealing with our casualties at their 4th & 5th Fd. Ambulances until that date. He also warned us of probable alteration in orders. . G/821/2nd Div.

3 p.m. 1st Corps Operation Order No.78 received.Secret No.G/76/12.

2nd Division to retain CUINCHY and GIVENCHY, we to take FESTUBERT and RUE DE L'EPINETTE as originally arranged, by 10 a.m. tomorrow.
4th Lon.Inf.Bde. remaining as our Reserve temporarily at LABEUVRIERE.
Spoke to 2nd Divn.on phone who agreed that tomorrow must be an error and they had referred to 1st Corps and were awaiting reply.
Meanwhile wired 5th Lon.Inf.Bde. cancelling orders for battalion to billet in ANNEQUIN tomorrow, and asked 1st Divn. for accommodation for 2 battalions 6th Lon.Inf.Bde. where they are now. . G.B/269.

2-45 p.m. 2nd Army report hostile columns on YPRES - WARNETON road moving South-east. G/745/1st C.

3-40 p.m. 1st Army report hostile Division moving on DOUAI - ARRAS road on LENS. . . G/747/1st C.

6-30 p.m. 1st Corps Operation Order No. 78, para 2, amended to read "10 a.m.,25th" instead of "10 a.m., tomorrow". . . G/749/1st C.

23rd April (contd).

6-45 p.m. 2nd Division Operation Order No. 36 cancelling No. 35, received.   Secret.   G/76/13.

This conforms to 1st Corps Operation Order No. 78 as above.

10-0 p.m. Divisional Operation Order No. 1   Attached.
issued, Secret, and completed by "A & Q"
wiring billets (ESSARS and LES FACONS & part
LE TOURET) to 6th Lon.Inf.Bde.

MENSECQ.   ## 24th April, 1915.

Slight frost - Bright morning.

Headquarters moved to Marche Aux Poulets BETHUNE, at 2 p.m.

Received - Artillery experiments in breaking
   down parapet with 18 pdr. H.E. successful.   G/318/1st C.
      Passed to Divl.Arty. Confidential.

      Instructions to practice assault   G.A/41/1st C.
from entrenchments.   .   .   Secret.   G/76/15.

9-30 p.m. 4th Lon.Inf.Bde. placed in Corps   G.A/42/1st C.
Reserve - Communicated to Brigade - Secret.   G/76/17.

Bi-carbonate of soda purchased; to be kept in trenches for purpose of soaking breathing pads to counter effect chlorine gases now used by enemy.

Copies of Defence Scheme 1st and 2nd Divisions received from 2nd Division.

BETHUNE.   ## 25th April, 1915.

Slight rain early morning.

6-6 a.m.   2nd Division report all quiet.

9-30 a.m. Reported to 1st Corps reliefs by 5th and 6th London Infantry Brigades completed.

10-20 a.m. Rear battalions of 5th and 6th London Infantry Brigades placed in Divisional Reserve. G.B/294.

Occupation of Trench line

OCCUPATION OF TRENCH LINE.

	RUE DE L'EPINETTE Section (D.1).			FESTUBERT Section (O).	
Sub-Sections.	d.	c.	b. a.	C.2 and 3.	C.1.
Firing Line.	3 Companies.		2 Companies.	2 Companies.	2 Companies.
Supporting Pts.	Post 14. (2 M.G's. (1 Secn. E.3. 1 Platoon.		Indian) 1 Coy. (2 Pltns (Garr) Village) (2 ,, (mobile) Post 14. 2 M.G's, 1 Secn.	Rue Du Cailloux – 2 Platoons. FESTUBERT 2 ,,	LE PLANTIN) 1 Coy. Posts E,D,B.)
H.Q. & Reserve.	RUE DU BOIS. H.Q.& 3 Platoons		RUE de l'EPINETTE. H.Q.& 1 Coy.	TUNING FORK (F.5.a). H.Q.& 1 Coy.	Breastworks (F.6.a). H.Q.& 1 Coy.
Brigade Reserve	LE TOURET Rue de l'EPINETTE.		H.Q.& 2 Coys.) 2 Companies.)	TUNING FORK (F.4.b). 2 Companies.) GORRE (East) . H.Q.& 2 Coys.)	
Divl. Reserve.	ESSARS. LES FAÇONS. MESPLAUX.		H.Q.& 1 Coy.) 1 Company.) 1 Company.)	GORRE (West). H.Q.& 2 Coys.) LACROIX de Fer. 1 Company.) ESSARS. 1 Company.)	
Brigade H.Q.	CSE de RAUX.			LOISNE.	
R.E.	4th Lon.Fd.Co. – LES GLAUGMES.			3rd Lon.Fd.Co. – GORRE.	
1st Line Inf.	21st, 22nd, 23rd – ESSARS.			17th,19th,20th – GORRE.	
Transport.	24th Bn. – LE TOURET.			18th Bn. – ESSARS.	
Artillery.	25th Fd.Arty.Bde. 18 Pdr. . 8th Lon.F.A. Bde. 5" Howr. . 4.5" Howr. . 15 Pdr. . 5th Lon.F.A.Bde.			36th Fd.Arty.Bde. (48 & 71 Batteries). 1 Secn.47th Batty. (44th F.A.Bde.). 15th,16th Battys (6th Lon.F.A.Bde). 19th Battery. (7th ,, ,,).	
Brigade Amm.Cols.	6th Lon.F.A.Bde. – Fm Du ROI.			7th Lon. F.A.Bde. – Distillery, BETHUNE.	
for S.A.A.	36th Brigade – ECLUSE D'ESSARS.				

25th April (contd).

Received - Instructions (2) re Operations. Secret.   G/289/1st C.25/4/15
    Copies to D.A., 5th & 6th Lon.Inf.Bdes. and 2nd   G/76/18.
    Divn. for 4th Gds.Bde.

5-40 p.m.   Progress reports - All quiet.   G.B./304.

Received - Instructions re hose pipes discovered
         protruding from enemy's trenches. Secret.   G/320/1st C.
    Circulated to D.A., 5th & 6th Lon.Inf.Bdes.   G/110.

         Air report 5-40 p.m. 4 trains at LA BASSEE.   G/776/1st C.
Forwarded to 5th and 6th Lon.Inf.Bdes.   G.H./312.

         1st Divn. leave R.A. personnel to work trench   Q/277/1st Div
mortars.   G.H./290.

     Progress Report.   Attached.

BETHUNE.   ## 26th April 1915.

Fine night - slight mist early morning.

5-30 a.m.   Quiet night reported.

Artillery situation, in amplification of yesterday's
Table -
     The guns supporting L'EPINETTE Section are
situated -
25th Bde. R.F.A.   North of RUE DU BOIS. About X 18.
13th & 14th Battys.(15 prs) ,, ,,   X 18,b & d.
8th Lon.F.A.Bde. (5" Hows). ,, ,,   X 18.
12th Batty.(15 prs).   RUE de L'EPINETTE. ,,   X 24.a.7.5.
     The above under command of 1st Division but firing on
our front. Grouped under O.C. 25th Bde.R.F.A. who is in direct
communication with H.Qrs.6th Lon.Inf.Bde; O.C. 5th and 8th Lon.
F.A.Bdes.affiliated.

Those supporting FESTUBERT Secn. are situated :-

36th F.A.Bde.,71st Batty.) near LE TOURET -   X 22.a.5.3.
         48th ,,) LOISNE Rd.   X 22.c.6.3.
15th Batty. (15 pdr).   East of ,,   X 28.b.5.5.
70th ,, (34th F.A.B.) ,, ,,   X 28.c.9.1.
16th & 19th (15 pdr).
Secn.47th Batty.(4.5" Howr).
     The above under our command. Grouped under O.C. 36th
Brigade R.F.A., who is in direct communication with H.Qrs. 5th
Lon.Inf.Brigade.   O.C. 6th Lon.F.A.Bde.affiliated.

     Principles of Defence of Sections issued.   G/111. Copy
                                                                   attached.
5-30 p.m.   All quiet reports.

     1st Division leave some R.A. personnel in
L'EPINETTE Section to work trench mortars.

     Additional 3 rounds per gun of 5th Lon.   B.M/637. D.A.
F.A.Bde. allowed for registration on our front.   G.B./319.
                                                                         Q/275/1st C.
                                                                        G.B/324.
                                                                        B.M/648. D.A.

26th April (contd).

Boundary between GIVENCHY and FESTUBERT Sections defined by traverse in new line of Breastworks to be marked by 4th Gds.Brigade. Interview with 2nd Division. . . G.H/323.

9 p.m. News of successful counter attacks by IInd Army and French East and North of YPRES received and circulated.

Arrangements made for each Platoon of Cyclist Company to do 48 hours in trenches. G.H./328.

Progress Report attached. Nothing unusual.

BETHUNE. 27th April 1915.

Fine night. Cold morning. Fine afternoon.

5-30 a.m. Quiet night reported. Searchlight on LA BASSEE Church.

5-50 a.m. 2nd Divn. report enemy more active and bombarding trenches at GIVENCHY.

2-52 p.m. 1st Army report French IXth Corps report now no Germans West of Canal (N of YPRES) except a Bridgehead at STEESTRAAT which is about to be attacked. Circulated.

7-50 p.m. Machine gun sections of 4th Lon.Inf.Bde. (Corps Reserve) ordered up. 2 detachments to 5th Lon.Inf.Bde. and 2 to 6th Lon.Inf.Bde. All concerned, including 1st Corps and 2nd Div. informed. . . . . . G.B.347 & 8.

Br.Gen.G.S. 1st Corps explained that one Secn. of 4" Trench Mortar Batty R.G.A. now in trenches of 6th Lon.Inf.Bde. were attached to us and at our disposal.

A portable searchlight handed over by 2nd Div. R.E. Allotted to 5th Lon.Inf.Bde.

G/90 & R.E/690
1st Div.
G.H/343 & 350.

5th Lon.F.A.Bde. placed definitely under our orders, to register for 1st Divn. by inter-Divl.arrangements. Result of pointing out that 1st Divn. were using their ammunition to register points for them and that up to last night (vide increased allowance of ammn asked for and sanctioned yesterday) they had not registered our defensive front. D.A. informed.

G/797/1st C.

G.H./345.

5-30 p.m. No change in situation. All quiet reported.

Progress report. Nothing noticeable. Attached.

10-45 p.m. Asked 1st Corps for use of 4 Machine Guns from Motor Machine Gun Battery. . G.B./354.

14.

27th April (contd).

10-55 p.m.   5th Lon.Inf.Bde. Divl.Reserve Battn. rendezvous
     at GORRE with H.Qrs.at that Church apptd.
6th Lon.Inf.Bde. Divl.Reserve Battn. rendezvous
     at LE TOURET with H.Qrs. at those cross roads
     appointed.
Plans of assembly and routes to be reconnoitred
and handed over to relieving battalions.
Battns ready to move at 2 hours notice; time to
reach rendezvous after receipt of orders to be
reported.   G.B/355.

    Squadron King Edwards Horse - Divl.Mounted
troops - which had gone to EQQUEDECQUES on
detrainment (25th) came up today to FONTENELLE Fm.

    4th Lon.Inf.Bde. and 4th Fd.Amb. (Corps
Reserve) are at LABEUVRIERE and LAPUGNOY.
5th Fd.Amb.carrying on washing and shops at
ALLOUAGNE. Divl.Cyclists in BETHUNE and Divl.
Ammn.Col. at ANNEZIN (really BETHUNE).
Train also in BETHUNE (refilling point).
Supply Column at LOZINGHEM.

BETHUNE.   ### 28th April 1915.

Fine night. Very fine clear morning.Hot day.

5-30 a.m.   Quiet night reported.

    G.O.C. inspected Div.Ammn.Col. and Squadron
King Edwards Horse.

5-30 p.m.   Quiet day reported.

8-10 p.m.   6th Lon.Inf.Bde. report time calculated for
Divl.Reserve Battns to reach Rendezvous - LE
TOURET - Ref. G.B.355 of yesterday.
2 Coys - 1 hour; 1 Coy - 1½ hours;
1 Coy. - 1¾ hours, after receipt of order to move.   B.M/441/6th Lo
                                                                 I.Bde.

    Progress report - nothing particular.   Attached.

BETHUNE.   ### 29th April, 1915.

Very fine night - hot.

5-30 a.m.   Quiet night reported.

    Divl.Mtd.Troops in Reserve - rendezvous at
LA MOTTE appointed.   G.H/378.

    All Divl.Reserves to be in readiness to move
at 2 hours notice by day and one hour's notice
by night.
    Paras. 5 (ii) and (iii) of G/111.Principles
of Defence redrafted and amendments issued.

    Distribution of Division in billets.   Attached.

5-30 p.m.   Quiet day reported.

29th April (contd).

Divl. Cyclists report they could be at rendezvous above in ½ hour.	G.203.
M.G. Detachments of 4th Lon.Inf.Bde. to be relieved every 48 hours.	G.B/376.
Machine Guns of battalions in Divl. Reserve to be with them and **NOT** in trenches.	G.B/377.

BETHUNE.   ## 30th April 1915.

5-30 a.m.   Quiet night reported.

Fine night, misty morning - very hot day.

5th Fd.Co.R.E. at our disposal on and after 3rd May. C.R.E. and 5th & 6th Lon.Inf. Bdes. informed.	G.B/397.
2nd Divn. will reconstruct work "E.3" in D.1. Section (EPINETTE).	G.B/400.
Hose pipes visible in front of D.1. ordered to be destroyed forthwith.	S.C/125. D.A. G.B/396. G/835 & 7/1stC G.B/399.

5-30 p.m.   Report no change in situation. Some shelling.

Progress Report - Nothing particular beyond reconnaissances (2) right up to German wire by 2nd Lt. E. Steele, 18th Bn. Lon.Regt.

Special report on Work "K" in enemy's lines A.3.a.3.3.

Received Secret - Maps of routes referred to in 2nd Divn.Secret Instructions, para 8, dated 23rd April 1915 (not received).   G/76/19.

Attached - Casualties for last days of march and month of April.
            40 Killed - 228 Wounded.

Sketch of dispositions in front line.

NOTE - It appears that the 2nd London Heavy Battery, which had been detached to Indian Corps on landing, was engaged ~~with~~ in the recent fighting at YPRES; from accounts to hand it was probably captured by the enemy during the first attack under cover of asphyxiating gases.

CASUALTIES — 25th MARCH to 30th APRIL 1915.

"K" = killed. "W" = wounded. "M" = missing.

OFFICERS NAMES, AND UNITS.

- Capt. E. Gore-Browne, 8th Battalion London Regiment.
- 2/Lieut. J.G. Gregory, 6th " " "
- Major H.H.S. Marsh, 4th Lon. Field Co. R.E. Died of wounds 2nd Apl. 1915.
- Major E.A. Myer, 6th Battalion London Regiment
- Lt. H.M. Rushworth, 7th Battalion London Regiment
- 2/Lieut. B.N. Nixon, 23rd Battalion London Regiment
- (Two of these reported as "Accidentally wounded".)
- Capt. L.R.E. West, 8th Bn. L.R. (K.) 2/Lieut. R.M. Maccabe (W. and died of wounds).
- * Reported as "accidentally killed".
- ° Two of these reported as "accidentally wounded".
- 2/Lieut. G. Davies, 24th Battalion London Regiment.
- x Transferring entry re Major H.H.S. Marsh, wounded Apl 1st. died of wounds Apl 2nd.

DATE 1915	OFFICERS K.	W.	M.	OTHER RANKS K.	W.	M.	TOTAL K.	W.	M.
Mch. 25		1			1			1	
27					1			2	
28				1			1		
29					8			8	
30					1			1	
31				1			1		
Apl. 1		1		1	2		1	3	
2	1			2	8		2	8	
3				2	10		2	10	
4				2	10		2	10	
5		1			4			5	
6				1			1		
7					6			6	
8				1	6		1	6	
9				1	5		1	5	
10				1	5		1	5	
11				1	3		1	3	
12				1	3		1	3	
13					4			4	
14				1	3		1	3	
15		1		2	16		2	17	
16				1	3		1	3	
17					1			1	
18					°4			4	
19				1	4		1	4	
20				3	9		3	9	
21				3	19		3	19	
22				3	13		3	13	
23	2			2	18		4	18	
24				2	3		2) 3		
25					5			5	
26				1	7		1	7	
27				*1	6		1	6	
28				2	°6		2	6	
29				2	9		2	10	
30		1		2	15		2	15	
	3	6		36	223		39	229	
x	1	1					x 1	1	
	4	5		36	223		40	228.	

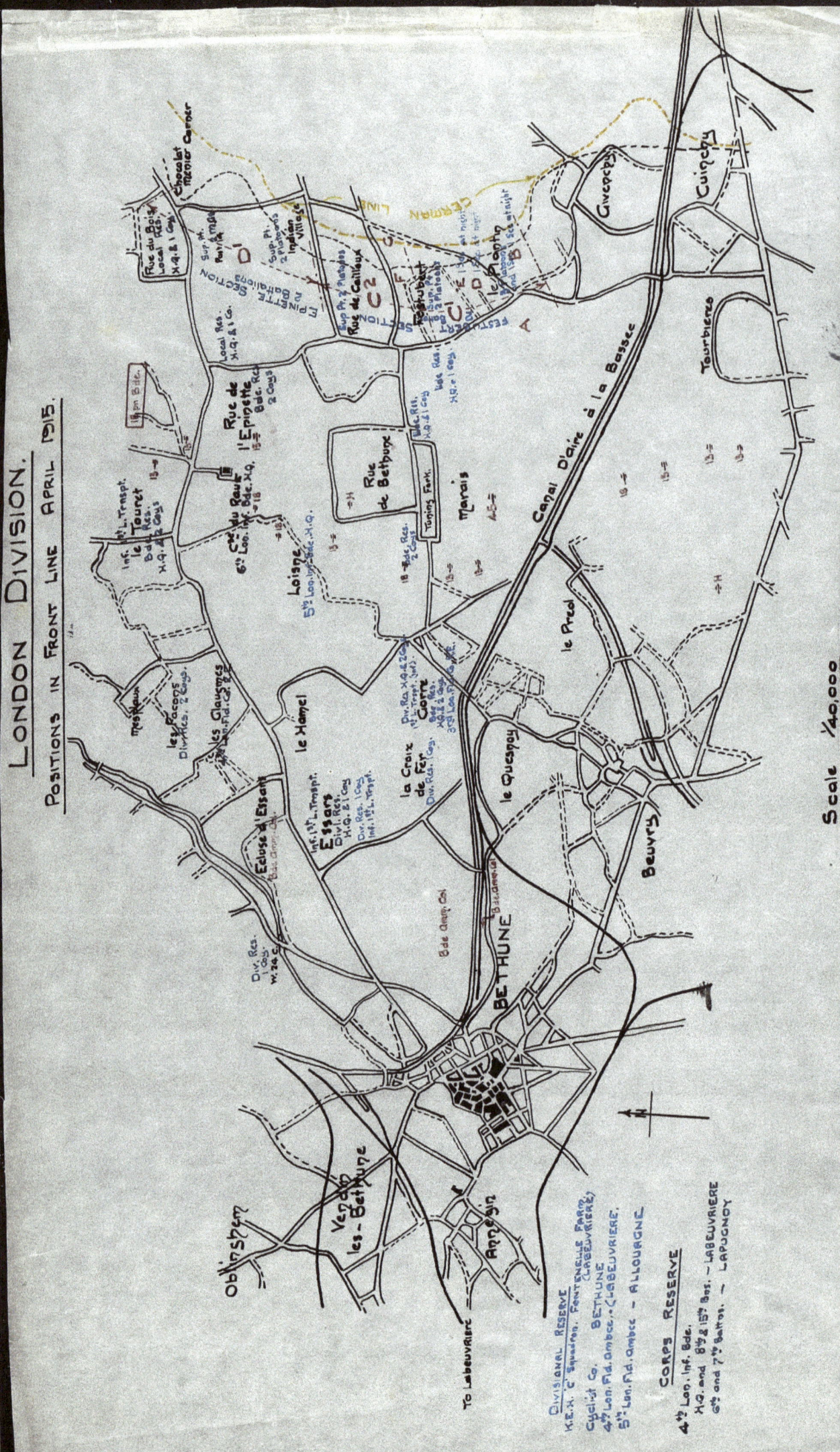

Wt. W1154/2240 7/11. 7,500,000. Sch. 4a. "A" Form.   Army Form C. 2121.

MESSAGES AND SIGNALS.

Prefix	Code	m.	Words	Charge	This message is on a/c of:	Rec'd. at	m.
Office of Origin and Service Instructions.			Sent			Date	
			At	m.	Service.	From	
			To			By	
			By		(Signature of "Franking Officer.")		

TO   1st   Corps

Sender's Number.	Day of Month	In reply to Number	
G.79.	First.	G.515	A A A

Cancel	1.G.77	from	this	Office.
add	Bns	to	join	First
Div.	will	be	21st	and
22nd	Lon.	Regt.	who	are
in	Billets	at	OBLINGHEM	and
VENDIN				

From: Second Lon Div
Place:
Time: 7·50 am

The above may be forwarded as now corrected.   (Z)

Censor. | Signature of Addresser or person authorised to telegraph in his name.

* This line should be erased if not required.

"A" Form. Army Form C. 2121.
MESSAGES AND SIGNALS.   No. of Message_____

Prefix	Code	m.	Words.	Charge.	This message is on a/c of:	Recd. at_____ m.
Office of Origin and Service Instructions.			Sent			Date_____
			At_____ m.		Service.	From_____
			To			
			By		(Signature of "Franking Officer.")	By_____

TO { fourth ...... Inf Bde
     fifth ...... "

| Sender's Number | Day of Month | In reply to Number | AAA |

Cancel 1098 of last night and two
battns of 6" London Inf Bde will go to
1st Divn as their present billets are
more suitably placed for the move

From 2nd London Divn
Place
Time

The above may be forwarded as now corrected. (Z)

Censor. Signature of Addressor or person authorised to telegraph in his name
* This line should be erased if not required.
(24473). M.R.Co.,Ltd. Wt.W4843/541. 50,000. 9/14. Forms C2121/10.

Wt. W1154/2240. 7/11. 7,500,000. Sch. 4a.		"A" Form.		Army Form C. 2121.

MESSAGES AND SIGNALS.

TO: Sixth Lon. Inf. Bde.

Sender's Number.	Day of Month	In reply to Number	
G. 81.	First		A A A

21st	and	22nd	Battalion	London
Regt.	selected	to go	to 1st	Div
on	2nd	April	aaa	
Warn	Bus	as	they	may
have	to	march	this	afternoon
aaa	Acknowledge			

From: 2nd Lon. Div.
Place:
Time: 7-50 am

"A" Form. Army Form C. 2121.
MESSAGES AND SIGNALS. No. of Message_____

| Prefix Code m. | Words. | Charge. | This message is on a/c of: | Recd. at m. |
| Office of Origin and Service Instructions. | Sent At m. To By | | _____ Service. (Signature of "Franking Officer.") | Date From By |

TO { Second Division

| Sender's Number | Day of Month | In reply to Number | |
| G.82 | First | | AAA |

Ref-	my	G.75	6th	Lon
Inf.	Bde	will	now	go
to	First	Division	aaa	Please
cancel	my	message	as	regards
Staff	of	that	Bde.	aaa
G.O.C.	5th	Lon	Inf	Bde
would	like	to	be	attached
with	his	Staff	for	a few
days	during	training	of-	his
Brigade.				

From Second Lon Div
Place
Time 9-10 am

The above may be forwarded as now corrected. (Z)

MESSAGES AND SIGNALS. — Army Form C. 2121. "A" Form.

TO: First Division

Sender's Number	Day of Month	In reply to Number	AAA
G. 85	First		

Ref 1st Corps No. 251/G of today aaa Wire destination of Battns and time you wish them to arrive aaa Can you also arrange for Brigadiers and Staff to be with one of the Brigades for a few days during the attachment aaa Wire to which Brigade they should go and where they should Billet

From: Second London Division
Time: 3.26 pm

Wt. W1154/2240. 7/11. 7,500,000. Sch. 4a.		"A" Form.		Army Form C. 2121.
		MESSAGES AND SIGNALS.		No. of Message_____

Prefix ___ Code ___ m.	Words	Charge	This message is on a/c of:	Recd. at ___ m.
Office of Origin and Service Instructions.				Date ___
	Sent		_____ Service.	From ___
	At ___ m.			
	To ___			By ___
	By ___		(Signature of "Franking Officer.")	

TO { 2 Lon Div

Sender's Number.	Day of Month	In reply to Number		
* No. 287	1st			A A A

Your G/2/6 received

2 LD G/75.
4-45pm

From: 6 Lon Inf Bde
Place:
Time: 4-30 pm

The above may be forwarded as now corrected. (Z)

Censor. Signature of Addressee or person authorised to telegraph in his name.

* This line should be erased if not required.

SIXTH LON INF BDE

G 86 First

Ref my G/2/6 today AAA One battalion billeting party report 3rd Brigade H.Q. RICHEBOURG ST VAAST 11 a.m. tomorrow AAA Battalion H.Q. and one company RICHEBOURG ST VAAST 5 p.m. AAA Remainder march via VIEILLE CHAPELLE reaching RICHEBOURG ST VAAST 6-30 p.m. AAA Second battalion billeting party report Guards Brigade H.Q. CHE DU RAUX SQR X 17 C 3-1 at 11 a.m. tomorrow AAA Remainder this battalion reach LE TOURET X 16 at 5-30 p.m. AAA Arrangements for Brigade Staff to visit units while attached will be notified later AAA Acknowledge

Second Lon Div

6-25 p.m

2nd London Division.
================

The 21st and 22nd London Battalions will proceed tomorrow, 2nd April, to join 1st Division.

Each of these battalions will be temporarily attached for a period of from 8 to 12 days, one to the 1st Brigade and one to the 3rd Brigade of 1st Division, under interdivisional arrangements.

The G.O.C. 1st Division will be good enough to give to the O.C. 6th London Brigade facilities to see his battalions when in front line.

The Lieut.General Commanding desires that each <u>platoon</u> shall do 24 hours duty in the trenches along with regular troops, and 24 hours in support. Each <u>company</u> should then be similarly placed alongside regular troops.

Platoons in reserve, i.e. those which have completed or are waiting their turn in the trenches, may be employed in digging or other necessary work, so that the whole battalion may be gaining useful experience daily.

On the assumption that 2 platoons can be accommodated daily in the firing line, it is calculated that the whole period of training for a battalion will last from 8 to 12 days.

No. 251/G.
1st April 1915.

(sd) R.Whigham,Br.Genl.
General Staff,
1st Corps.

(2)

6th Lon.Inf.Bde.
================

For information and retention. *Acknowledge by wire. Time of move and destination will be wired to you as soon as ascertained.*

(Sd) B.F. Burnett-Hitchcock
Major,
General Staff,
2nd London Division, T.F.

1st Corps No. 251 (G).

~~1st Division.~~
1/2nd London Division.

The 21st and 22nd London Battalions will proceed tomorrow, 3rd April, to join 1st Division.

Each of these battalions will be temporarily attached for a period of from 8 to 12 days, one to the 1st Brigade and one to the 3rd Brigade of 1st Division, under interdivisional arrangements.

The G.O.C. 1st Division will be good enough to give to the O.C. 6th London Brigade facilities to see his battalions when in front line.

The Lieut.General Commanding desires that each platoon shall do 24 hours duty in the trenches along with regular troops, and 24 hours in support. Each company should then be similarly placed alongside regular troops.

Platoons in reserve, i.e. those which have completed or are awaiting their turn in the trenches, may be employed in digging or other necessary work, so that the whole battalion may be gaining useful experience daily.

On the assumption that 2 platoons can be accomodated daily in the firing line, it is calculated that the whole period of training for a battalion will last from 8 to 12 days.

1st April, 1915.

Robinson Brig.General,
General Staff, 1st Corps.

SUBJECT. <u>Instruction of Territorial Battalions.</u>

2nd London Division.

<u>6th London Battalion.</u> (attached 6th Brigade).

One company in front line of "A"2, as a whole company-
Another still doing individual trench instruction in "A"1.
Both companies under the command of O.C."A"1.

<u>7th London Battalion.</u> (attached 5th Brigade).

Instruction same as yesterday, a change of companies today.

<u>8th P.O. Rifles.</u>
One ~~section~~ company in "B"3 last night.

1st April 1915.   Forwarded for information.
                   Louis Vaughan Lt Col
                   for Major-General.
                   Commanding 2nd Division.

<u>2</u>

4th Lon Inf. Bde

For information and return.

                                    Lt. Colonel
                                    GENERAL STAFF
                                    2nd LONDON DIVISION.

P.T.O.

HEADQUARTERS
2ND LONDON DIVISION.

Noted and returned.

G. Cuthbert
Brig: General
Comdg 4th London Inf. Brigade

BRIGADE OFFICE
No. BM/118
2 - APR. 1915
4TH LONDON INFANTRY BRIGADE

1. One Battalion 2nd London Division will be attached to 1st Brigade from 2nd April for instructional purposes.

   The companies will be attached as follows:—

   <u>A Company</u> to 1st Bn. Coldstream Guards till the 3rd April. After that date to 1st Bn. Scots Guards.

   <u>B Company</u> to 1st Black Watch.

   <u>C Company</u> to 1st Cameron Highlanders.

   <u>D Company</u> to London Scottish.

2. In left subsection of D1 and in D2 and D3 one platoon will be attached to each of the three Companies in the defensive line, and the other platoon to the Company in support.

   The platoons will not be split up, and will always remain with the same Company, going into the defensive line or in support with that Company.

   The Captain of the Company will be attached to one Company during the whole period of training.

   In right subsection of D1 two platoons will be attached to the Company in the defensive line, one platoon to the Company in INDIAN village, and one platoon to one of the Companies in Brigade Reserve.

3. The Battalion Headquarters will be attached to Scots Guards but will be billetted near GLAUGMES.

4. The Machine Guns Sections will be billetted with their Battalion Headquarters at GLAUGMES, and will be attached to the Machine Guns detachments throughout the Section under instructions which will be issued by Brigade Machine Gun officer.

5. All transport will remain with Battalion Headquarters at GLAUGMES.

6. Battalions will take over the rations for the companies attached to them from the Q.M. of the Battalion of 2nd London Division at the Refilling point at GLAUGMES.

7. Guides from each Battalion will meet the companies at LE TOURET at 5.30 p.m. tomorrow.

8. Officers Commanding Battalions will give all the help they can to give useful instruction to the units attached. As far as possible these will do their share of the ordinary trench work, working parties &c.

Major
Brigade Major, 1st Guards Bde.

Headquarters

1st Division.

With reference to previous correspondence regarding the attachment of Officers and N.C.O's to the 2nd and 3rd Brigades, it is notified that the last party from the 5th London Infantry Brigade will return on Monday 5th instant, and the first party from the 6th London Infantry Brigade (23rd and 24th Lon.Battalions) will go up for instruction on that day, under similar arrangements as for the former brigade.

2.L.D.G/2/7
2nd April 1915.

for Major General,
Commanding 2nd London Division.

Copy   9/2/7

Headquarters,

    6th London Infantry Brigade.
    _____

    Parties of fifteen Officers and fifteen Non Commissioned Officers from the 23rd and 24th Battalions London Regiment, will be attached to the 2nd and 3rd Brigades, 1st Division, for a tour in the trenches of 24 hours each, commencing on Monday 5th instant.

    Busses will be provided to take them to their destinations daily and will wait to bring back parties who have completed their tour.

    Number One Bus, six Officers and six Non Commissioned Officers, will be met at LA COUTURE Church at 5.45 p.m. by representative of 3rd Brigade who will take party to Headquarters.

    Number two Bus, with remainder of party will be met by representative Second Brigade at Road junction at LE TOURET, Map Square X 16 at the same hour.

    No transport is available and parties will take rations and such kit only as they can carry themselves to the trenches.

    Two Busses will be parked in your Brigade Area on Monday 5th, please detail starting point for the parties and notify the same to this office.

    It is advisable to detail an additional N.C.O. to proceed with each bus to ensure that the party returning from the trenches is picked up.

    Fifteen Officers and N.C.Os. from the 5th London Infantry Brigade proceed to the trenches on Sunday and will return on Monday evening in the busses which have carried your first parties.

    Please inform me as early as possible of the date on which all Officers in these Battalions will have completed a tour.

                                            A.R. Hunt
2 L.D./2/7/G.   Captain,
2nd April, 1915.   General Staff,
                                         2nd London Division.

Copy

Headquarters
    5th Lon.Inf.Brigade.

        Reference your wire B.M. 140 of this day, please arrange for the two Motor Busses to proceed to the Headquarters of the 6th London Infantry Brigade on Monday 5th April to convey parties of Officers and N.C.O's from that Brigade to the 2nd and 3rd Brigades as has been done hitherto.   These busses will return on Monday night with your last party and will then be entirely at the disposal of the 6th London Infantry Brigade.

                                              H.R. Hunt
                                                Captain,
                                              General Staff
                                          2nd London Division, T.F.

1st Corps No. 251 (G).

~~2nd Division.~~

2nd London Division.
----

1. With reference to 1st Corps No. 251 (G), dated 24th March, the three battalions of the 2nd London Division now with 2nd Division will rejoin the 2nd London Division on the morning/~~evening~~ of the 7th instant.

2. Three more battalions will join the 2nd Division on the evening of the 7th instant. Inter-divisional arrangements will be made for the march and billets of these battalions.

3. The G.O.C. 2nd London Division will inform Corps Headquarters which battalions are selected.

2nd April, 1915.

R. Whigham Brig. General.
S.G.S.O., 1st Corps.

Message G.98 4 & 5 Bdes
"   G.99 1st Corps & 2 Div.

MESSAGES AND SIGNALS. Army Form C. 2121.

"A" Form.

TO: 2D Inf. Div.

Sender's Number: G.535 Day of Month: 3 AAA

The parties of Officers around the new attached to 1st Div should be withdrawn immediately now that 1st Div has two London Bns aaa addressed 2nd Inf Div Repeated 2nd Div

220/110.
10-11 pm

From: 1st Corps
Time: 10-5 pm

FOURTH LON INF BDE
FIFTH LON INF BDE

X. G. 110   Third

15th 17th and 18th London Battalions should reach BETHUNE on 7th April from 3 p.m. onwards and will billet there 15th in ECOLE DE JEUNES FILLES 17th in MONTMORENCY barracks 18th in ORPHANAGE AAA Billeting parties to report to town commander 88 RUE SADI CARNOT at 11 a.m. 7th April AAA Battalions will be attached 15th to 4th Bde 17th to 5th Bde 18th to 6th Bde AAA Commanding Officers should report for instructions at Hdqrs of Bde to which battalion is attached on afternoon 7th AAA Acknowledge

Second Lon Div

10-5 a.m.

SUBJECT. **Instruction of Territorial Battalions.**

2nd London Division.

6th London Battalion. (attached 6th Brigade.)

    Now holding "A"2 with a different company.

7th London Battalion (attached 5th Brigade)

    4th Company took over portion of line.
    Working party employed digging communication trench.

8th P.O. Rifles.

    This battalion took over "B"3. Instruction in the use of loopholes and firing over parapet in event of an attack. They took 25 hurdles out to No.4 GROUSE BUTT, but work was much interrupted by flares. 1 section R.E. and 1 section Territorial R.E. began the deviation in the breastwork.

3/4/15.

                                      Major-General.

                               Commanding 2nd Division.

4th Lon.Inf.Bde.
================

                For information and return

                                    Lt.Colonel,
                                    General Staff
                            2nd London Division, T.F.

P.T.O

3

HEADQUARTERS
2ND LONDON DIVISION.

Noted & returned.

G. Cuthbert.

Brig: General
Comdg 4th London Inf. Brigade

Headquarters 2nd Lon Division.

In reference to Div Routine order No 8 para 2 — is the route by which the units of this Brigade will move on the change of billets on April 7th is as follows. Reference maps France BETHUNE 1/40,000 & ARRAS Sheet 7 1/80,000

(1) 6th 7th 8th Battns Lon Regt. cross roads immediately S.W of ANNEZIN church — LABEUVRIÈRE thence along the N side of the railway to MARLE LES MINES — No 5 AUCHEL.

(2) The 15th Battn from CAUCHY — AUCHEL — No 5 at S end of AUCHEL — MARLE LES MINES — railway crossing just S of 2 in Square 20 — thence along the Southern side of the Railway — LABEUVRIÈRE — cross roads immediately SW of ANNEZIN church.

G. Cuthbert
Brig: General
Comdg 4th London Inf. Brigade

"A" Form. Army Form C. 2121.

MESSAGES AND SIGNALS.

Prefix	Code	m.	Words	Charge	This message is on a/c of:	Recd. at ___ m.
Office of Origin and Service Instructions.			Sent		___ Service.	Date ___
			At ___ m.			From
			To			By
			By		(Signature of "Franking Officer.")	

TO { 1st Corps
     1st Div. }

Sender's Number.	Day of Month	In reply to Number	
* G.H. 117.	4th		AAA

Ref. 1st Corps G.535 Busses will arrive LETOURET and LACOUTURE 5.45pm to bring back party now attached aaa Address 1st Div. repeated 1st Corps

From Second Lon Div.
Place
Time 10.15 am.

MESSAGES AND SIGNALS.

TO: 2 Lon. Div

Sender's Number: G.537
Day of Month: 4th
AAA

Ref G.535 Please arrange for Motor Busses to call for them tomorrow at Letouret and Lacouture and inform me 1st Div. at what time they may expect the busses.

21D/112.
12-27 am

From: 1st Corps

2nd London Division.

6th London Battalion. (attached 6th Brigade.)

6th London hold A.2. with one company, who built parados in that section. The other company carried out bricking of communication trenches.

7th London Battalion. (attached 5th Brigade).

Company took over left of C.1.

8th Post Office Rifles (attached 4th Brigade).

At work on GROUSE BUTTS, double revetting.

Louis Vaughan Lt Col
for
                Major-General,
4th April, 1915.   Commanding 2nd Division.

2

4th Lon. Inf. Bde.

For information and return.

Lt Colonel
GENERAL STAFF
2nd LONDON DIVISION.

HEADQUARTERS 3
2ND LONDON DIVISION.

Noted & returned.

G. Cuthbert.

Brig: General
Comdg 4th London Inf. Brigade

MESSAGES AND SIGNALS.

Army Form C. 2121.

TO: 6th Lon Inf Bde

Sender's Number: G.H.118. Day of Month: 4th AAA

No further attachment of Officers and NCO's to 1st Div. will be made ada. Cancel my G.2/7 of second inst.

From: 2 Lon Div
Time: 10-15 am

2nd London Division.

6th London Battn. (attached 5th Brigade.)

Held section A.2. until 3 p.m., when they were relieved by 5th Liverpools.

7th London Battn. (attached 5th Brigade.)

Instruction, which was the same as yesterday is now completed.

8th London Battn. (attached 4th Brigade).

Work on new breastwork (SCOTTISH TRENCH).

Louis Vaughan Lt Col
for
Major-General,
5th April, 1915.   Commanding 2nd Division.

4th Lon.Inf.Bde.
================

For information and return.

Lt.Colonel
GENERAL STAFF
2nd LONDON DIVISION.

Noted and returned.

G. Cuthbert
Brig: General
Comdg 4th London Inf. Brigade

HEADQUARTERS
2ND LONDON DIVISION.

Noted & returned.

Brig: General
Comdg 4th London Inf. Brigade

Copy No. 10

1st Division Order No. 76.

5th April 1915.

1. The 2nd Infantry Brigade will relieve the 3rd Infantry Brigade in Section "E" during the night of 7th - 8th April under arrangements to be made direct between General Officers Commanding the Brigades concerned.

These arrangements must ensure that troops in Reserve do not move off until other troops have actually arrived to relieve them.

2. On relief the 3rd Infantry Brigade will become 1st Corps Reserve, and will be in readiness to move at 2 hours notice.

3. On relief the 3rd Infantry Brigade will take over the billeting area now occupied by the 2nd Infantry Brigade, except the billets of the 9th Battalion The King's Liverpool Regiment at LES FACONS and MESPLAUX.

The 22nd London Battalion, now attached to the 3rd Infantry Brigade, will be billeted in LA COUTURE for the night 7th - 8th April, under arrangements to be made by the 3rd Infantry Brigade.

4. The 22nd London Battalion will rejoin the 2nd London Division on the morning of 8th April, under arrangements which will be communicated later.

E.S. Hoare Nairne
Lieut. Colonel.
General Staff, 1st Division.

Issued at 7 p.m. to :-

1st, 2nd and 3rd Infantry Brigades, 1st D.A., 1st D.E., Div. Mtd. Troops, A.D.M.S., "Q"., 2nd Divn., and 2nd London Division (for information), War Diary and file.

6th Lon.Inf.Bde.
===================

For information and return.

Lt.Colonel
GENERAL STAFF
2nd LONDON DIVISION.

[Stamp: GENERAL STAFF 2ND LONDON DIVISION / No. / 6 - APR.1915 / TERRITORIAL FORCE]

Memo. to 6 Bde. G.H./122
& Copy to Q

6th Lon.Inf.Bde.
================

    Herewith two copies of the 1st Guards Brigade Orders regarding the attachment of the 23rd Battalion to that Brigade from 11th instant.

    Kindly acknowledge receipt hereon.

                             Major,
                             General Staff,
                        2nd London Division T.F.

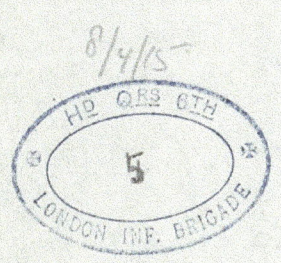

2

H. Qr. 2nd Lon. Div.

Received

8/4/15

MESSAGES AND SIGNALS. 9/2/6

TO: First Division

Sender's Number: G.H. 123
Day of Month: Sixth
AAA

Understand Twenty second London Regt. return to its billets morning eighth inst and Twenty first London Regt. morning of eleventh aaa Am instructed by First Corps that another battalion is to replace Twenty first aaa Propose sending Twenty third Battalion aaa What day should they join and when

From: Second Lon Div
Time: 9-20 am.

Wt. W1154/2240. 7/11. 7,500,000. Sch. 4a.		"A" Form.		Army Form C. 2121.

MESSAGES AND SIGNALS.   No. of Message_____

Prefix....... Code.......m.	Words	Charge	This message is on a/c of:	Recd. at.......m.
Office of Origin and Service Instructions.	Sent			Date............
....	At.......m.		............Service.	From............
....	To			By............
	By		(Signature of "Franking Officer.")	

TO	Second	Lon.	Div.	

Sender's Number.	Day of Month	In reply to Number	AAA
* G.577	6th	G.H. 123	

Yes	aaa	Twenty third	battn	
should	join	1st	Guards	Bde
on	eleventh	as	follows	aaa
Companies	to	be	at	road
junction	LE TOURET	at	6 pm	
aaa	HQrs	and	first	line
Transport	to	billets	in	X 14 C
during	afternoon	aaa	Supplies	to
come	up	with	1st	Guard
Bde	supplies	in	afternoon	when
they	will	be	distributed	
among	the	battalion	to	which
the	Companies	will	be	attached
		2nd/118		
		11-56 am		

From	1st	Div.		
Place				
Time	11-30 am			

The above may be forwarded as now corrected.   (Z)

Censor.   Signature of Addressor or person authorised to telegraph in his name.

* This line should be erased if not required.

"A" Form. Army Form C. 2121.

MESSAGES AND SIGNALS.   No. of Message _____

Prefix ____ Code ____ m. | Words. | Charge. | This message is on a/c of: | Recd. at ____ m.
Office of Origin and Service Instructions. | Sent At ____ m. To ____ By ____ | | Service. (Signature of "Franking Officer.") | Date ____ From ____ By ____

TO { 6th ___ ... ___ Bde

Sender's Number: GA 125 | Day of Month: Sixth | In reply to Number | AAA

Following received from First Div aaa Twenty third London Batty should join First Guards Brigade on eleventh as follows aaa Companies to be at road junction LE TOURET at 6 pm aaa Hdqrs and first line Transport to billets in X 11 C during afternoon aaa Supplies to come up with First Guards Bde supplies in afternoon when they will be distributed among the battalions to which the companies will be attached aaa Acknowledge

From Second Lon Div
Place
Time 12·30 pm

The above may be forwarded as now corrected. (Z)

Censor.   Signature of Addresser or person authorised to telegraph in his name

* This line should be erased if not required.

1st Div'n   G.H. 123

Understand 22nd Sqn Battn returns to
its billets morning of 8th inst. and 21st Sqn
Battn morning of 11th inst. AAA Am
instructed by 1st Corps that another
battalion is to replace 21st AAA Propose
sending 23rd Battalion AAA What day
should they join and where.

"A" Form.   Army Form C. 2121.

MESSAGES AND SIGNALS.   No. of Message _____

Prefix ___ Code ___ m	Words	Charge	This message is on a/c of:	Recd. at ___ m.
Office of Origin and Service Instructions				Date ___
	Sent		_____ Service.	From ___
	At ___ m			
	To ___			By ___
	By ___		(Signature of "Franking Officer.")	

| TO | 1st | Corps |
| | 2nd | Div |

| Sender's Number. | Day of Month. | In reply to Number | AAA |
| S.H.132 | 6 | | |

15 Bn B. Lon Regt leave RAIMBERT at 11-30 am tomorrow for BETHUNE marching via LABEUVIERE and Cross Roads South west of ANNEZIN CHURCH aaa 17 & 18 Bn leave BURBURE at 11 am for BETHUNE via PONT DU REVEILLON and CHOCQUES aaa 19 & 20 leave ALLOUAGNE at 2 pm for BETHUNE via REVEILLON and CHOCQUES aaa add 1st Corps Repeated 2nd Div

From: 2 Lon Div
Place:
Time: 10.25 pm

"A" Form. Army Form C. 2121.
MESSAGES AND SIGNALS.

| TO | 2 | Lon | Div | |

| Sender's Number. | Day of Month. | In reply to Number | AAA |
| G. 557 | 6th | | |

You	will	send	up	five
Batts	in	place	of	three
tomorrow	afternoon	to	be	attached
to	2nd	Divn	aaa	2nd
Div	have	been	asked	to
inform	you	billets	for	these
Batts		addressed	2	L Div
Repeated	2nd	Div.		

From: 1st Corps.
Time: 10-10 pm

"A" Form.
Army Form C. 2121.

MESSAGES AND SIGNALS.

No. of Message _____

Prefix	Code	m	Words	Charge	This message is on a/c of:	Recd. at _____ m.
Office of Origin and Service Instructions			Sent			Date _____
			At _____ m		_____ Service.	From _____
			To		(Signature of "Franking Officer.")	By _____
			By			

TO { 5 Lon Inf Bde

Sender's Number.	Day of Month.	In reply to Number	AAA
GB. 133	6		

Warn	19	and	20	Bn
to	move	tomorrow	7th	to
BETHUNE	for	attachment	to	Second
Div.	in	addition	to	17
and	18	Bn.	aaa	Route
as	for	17	& 18	Bn
aaa	Time	of	march	2 pm
aaa	Acks.			

From 2 L. Div.
Place
Time 10·25 pm

"A" Form.
MESSAGES AND SIGNALS.

Army Form C. 2121.

TO	2	Lon	Div	

Sender's Number.	Day of Month.	In reply to Number	AAA
G.H. 74	6th	G.H. 132	

19. Bn will be attached 5th Bde and 20th Bn to 6th Bde aaa Please direct Offrs Commdg to report at Bde H.Q. tomorrow afternoon for instns. aaa Billeting parties will report to Town Com'dt Bethune at 11 am tomorrow aaa Addd 2 L. Div Rep'd 1st Corps.

From 2nd Div.
Place
Time 11-25 pm

"A" Form.
Army Form C. 2121.

MESSAGES AND SIGNALS.
No. of Message

Prefix...Code...m	Words	Charge	This message is on a/c of:	Recd. at...m
Office of Origin and Service Instructions	Sent			Date
	At...m		...Service.	From
	To		(Signature of "Franking Officer.")	By

| TO | 6 | | | |

| Sender's Number. | Day of Month. | In reply to Number | AAA |
| G.H.127 | 6 | | |

G.H.125	In	Continuation	of	my
return	Twenty	first	Batt	will
Further	to	billets	on	eleventh
Later.	details	will	be	notified

From 2d Lon Div
Place
Time 2-45 pm

"A" Form.
MESSAGES AND SIGNALS.
Army Form C. 2121.

TO { Sixth Lon Inf Bde

Sender's Number: G.H.131
Day of Month: Sixth
AAA

Ref G.H.127 Twenty second Batt return from Trenches on eighth inst and will NOT be replaced by another Battn

From: Second Lon Div
Place:
Time: 6-40 pm

"A" Form.   Army Form C. 2121.

MESSAGES AND SIGNALS.   No. of Message_____

Prefix	Code	m	Words	Charge	This message is on a/c of:	Recd. at	m.
Office of Origin and Service Instructions			Sent			Date	
			At	m.	Service.	From	
			To				
			By		(Signature of "Franking Officer.")	By	

TO	5	Lon	Inf	Bde.

Sender's Number.	Day of Month.	In reply to Number	AAA
G.B. 134	7th	Bm 185	

Ref	my	G.B. 133	aaa	definite
orders	having	now	been	received
the	19	and	20	Bm
will	proceed	as	therein	warned
aaa	Your	Bde	HQ	may
move	to	Bethune	if you	can
arrange	necessary	accommodation	there	
aaa	19th	will	be	attached
to	5 Bde	and	20th	to
6th	Bde.	aaa	O.C.'s	to
report	at	these	Bde HQ	this
afternoon	for	orders	aaa	Billeting
parties	report	to	Town	Com at
Bethune	at	11 am	today	Clerk

From 2 Lon. Div.
Place
Time 7-36 am

The above may be forwarded as now corrected.   (Z)

C O P Y.
S E C R E T.

Copy No. 6.

1st Corps No.289.(G)

GENERAL STAFF 2ND LONDON DIVISION
No. G/76
6 - APR. 1915
TERRITORIAL FORCE

1st Army.
─────────

1. In accordance with instructions given me personally by the G.O.C. 1st Army, I submit the following general proposals for breaking the enemy's line and advancing eastwards through LORGIES.

2. The 1st Division will attack from our breastworks in front of RICHEBOURG L'AVOUE on a front of about 1,700 yards. Two brigades will carry out the assault on the enemy's front line, with a third brigade in divisional reserve.

3. Two brigades of the 2nd Division and one brigade of the 2nd London Division will be held in Corps Reserve, in positions of readiness about the RUE DU BOIS and INDIAN VILLAGE (Map squares S.14 and S.20).

4. The First Corps front from its junction with the French at CUINCHY to "CHOCOLAT MENIER CORNER" (Map square S.14.b.) will be held by one brigade 2nd Division (CUINCHY and GIVENCHY) and two brigades 2nd London Division (GIVENCHY exclusive to CHOCOLAT MENIER CORNER).

5. The first objective of the two brigades entrusted with the assault will be the road running from LA QUINQUE RUE to the NEUVE CHAPELLE - LA BASSEE road. Thence the attack will be directed on RUE DU MARAIS and LORGIES, the advance being carried out rather in echelon from the left, the strong point at GIVENCHY being the pivot of the movement as it progresses.

6. The reasons for initiating the attack from the breastworks in front of RICHEBOURG L'AVOUE in preference to those south of CHOCOLAT MENIER CORNER are :-
   (i) The German second line trenches opposite RICHEBOURG L'AVOUE face rather south-west, present a flank to RICHEBOURG L'AVOUE.
   (ii) Close co-operation with the attack of the Indian Corps on the FERME DU BIEZ will be facilitated.

7. To enable the necessary preparations to be made and to give some rest to the troops of the 1st Division, I request that the Indian Corps may take over the left section of the line now held by the 1st Division as far south as "The Orchard" inclusive (Map square S.10.a., but see also 1/5,000 map for position of "The Orchard") as soon as convenient.

8. Of the Army Artillery now at the disposal of 1st Corps, the 26th Heavy Battery will be required in its present position to support the CUINCHY - GIVENCHY front. Two of the batteries of the 44th Brigade R.F.A. (Hows) will be required also on this front to deal with counter-attacks, but can support our main attack by firing on RUE d'OUVERT.

9. If the French would agree to take over the CUINCHY section of the line at present held by the 1st Corps, two additional battalions would be released for offensive purposes.

Please acknowledge receipt by wire.

6.30 a.m.
7th April, 1915.

(Sd) C.C.Monro   Lieut-General,
Commanding 1st Corps,

1. The 2/5 Bn, 2nd London Division will be attached to 1st Brigade from 11th April for instructional purposes.
   The companies will be attached as follows:-
   <u>A Company</u> to 1st Bn Coldstream Guards.
   <u>B Company</u> to 1st Black Watch.
   <u>C Company</u> to 1st Cameron Highlanders.
   <u>D Company</u> to London Scottish.

2. In left subsection of D1 and in D2 and D3 one platoon will be attached to each of the three Companies in the defensive line, and the other platoon to the Company in support. The platoons will not be split up, and will always remain with the same company going into the defensive line or in support with that Company.
   The Captain of the Company will be attached to one Company during the whole period of training.
   In right subsection of D1 two platoons will be attached to the company in the defensive line, one platoon to the company in INDIAN Village, and one platoon to one of the companies in Brigade Reserve.

3. The Battalion Headquarters will be attached to Black Watch but will be billeted near LES SLAUSMES at X.14.c.5.3.

4. The Machine Gun Sections will be billeted with their Battalion Headquarters at LES GLAUSMES and will be attached to the Machine Gun detachments throughout the Sections under instructions which will be issued by Brigade Machine Gun Officer. Battn Machine Gun Officer should be at Brigade Headquarters X.14.C.3 at 10. a.m. on 8th April.

5. All transport will remain with Battalion Headquarters at LES GLAUSMES.

6. Battalions will take over the rations for the companies attached to them from the Q.M. of the Battalion of 2nd London Division at the Refilling Point at LES GLAUSMES.

7. Guides from each Battalion will meet the companies at LE TOURET at 6 p.m. 8th April.

8. Billeting parties will meet the Staff Captain at road junction in X.20.B.6.2. at 10 a.m. on 8th April.

9. Officers Commanding Battalions will give all the help they can give useful instruction to the units attached. As far as possible these will do their share of the ordinary trench work, working parties, &c.

7/4/18

R. L. Bowlby
Major.
Brigade Major 1st Guards Bde.

6th Lon.Inf.Bde.
========================

  Herewith two copies of the 1st Guards Brigade Orders regarding the attachment of the 23rd Battalion to that Brigade from 11th instant.

  Kindly acknowledge receipt hereon.

             Major,
            General Staff,
          2nd London Division T.F.

Penetrating wound, jaw with shock.

S E C R E T.

COPY NO. 3.

FIRST CORPS OPERATION ORDER NO. 76.

8th April, 1915.

1.   Instructions have been received to the effect that the Indian Corps will, on the nights of 11th/12th and 12th/13th April, take over the front line from 1st Corps as far south as the ORCHARD (inclusive) about 400 yards S.W. of PORT ARTHUR. The relief will be completed by the morning of the 13th instant.

    Arrangements for the above relief will be made between 1st Division and Meerut Division.

2.   The relief of the Artillery will be carried out on the night of the 13th/14th under interdivisional arrangements.

3.   The attached sketch shows the new dividing line between 1st and Indian Corps.

4.   The 1st Division will report progress of reliefs as they take place.

Hereward Wake

Major,
General Staff, 1st Corps.

Issued at 3:30 p.m.

Copies to :-
    1st Division.
    2nd Division.
    2nd London Division.
    Indian Corps.
    No.3 Squadron R.F.C.

SUBJECT:- INSTRUCTION TERRITORIAL BATTALIONS.

2nd London Division.

18th and 20th London Battalions. (attached 6th Brigade).
   1 company 18th London attached to K.R.R. in "A"1.
   1 ,, 20th ,, ,, ,, 1st Berks, in "A"3.
   18th London battalion employed on bricking communication trenches.

17th and 19th London Battalions. (attached 5th Brigade)
   17th London attached to Worcestershire Regt in "C"2.
   19th ,, ,, ,, Oxford & Bucks.L.I. in "C"1.

15th London Battalion. (attached 4th Brigade).
   1 company 15th London doing general work during the day.
   1 company 15th London goes into the trenches tonight, and will be disposed as follows:-

      ½ company in "B:3.
      1 platoon in "B"2.
      1 platoon in "B"1.

C.O. and Adjutant attached to O.C. "B"1 for the night.

8th April 1915.
                      Brig-General.
                      Commanding 2nd Division.

2nd London Division.

18th & 20th London Battns. (attached 6th Brigade.)

18th and 20th London in trenches in A.1 and A.3. respectively.

17th & 19th London Battns. (attached 5th Brigade.)

2 Coys, 19th London.   )
1 Coy, 17th London.   ) Extended along front.

17th London employed in two reliefs each of 100 men.

15th London Battalion. (attached 4th Brigade.)

15th London, all usefully employed.

Louis Vaughan Lt Col
for
Brigadier-General,
Commanding 2nd Division.

10th April, 1915.

2.

Fourth) Lon.Inf.Bdes.
Fifth)

For information and retention.

(Sd) B.B.H. Major
for Lt.Colonel,
General Staff,
Second Lon. Div.

11th April 1915.
2 L.D. 2/8/G.

Subject:- <u>Instruction of Territorial Battalions.</u>

2nd London Division.

<u>18th & 20th London Battalions</u> (attached 6th Brigade.)

Have one company each attached for trench duties to A.1 and A.3. respectively.
Remainder digging.

<u>17th and 19th London Battalions</u> (attached 5th Brigade.)

One company spread along front in C.1.
One company spread along front in C.2.
Each battalion provided working party of 100 men.

<u>15th London Battalion</u> (attached 4th Brigade.)

Employed in trenches by platoons and at work by companies.

11-4-15.

F. A. Buzzard Major G.S.
for Brigadier-General,
Commanding 2nd Division.

Copy to 4 & 5th Bde.

SUBJECT. Training of Territorial Battalions.

2nd London Division.

18th & 20th London Battalions. (attached 6th Brigade).

Employed as yesterday.

17th & 19th London Battalions. (attached 5th Brigade).

1 company of the 17th) took up portions allotted to one
1   ,,   ,, ,, 19th) of our companies.

15th London Battalion. (attached 4th Brigade.)

Employed as per programme. C.O. given fullest orders and instructions as to holding "B"1, tomorrow night.

12th April 1915.

Louis Vaughan Lt Col
for   Brig-General.
Commanding 2nd Division.

2.

Fourth
Fifth   Lon.Inf.Bdes.

For information and retention.

Major,
General Staff,
Second Lon. Div.

13th April 1915.
2 L.D.No.2/8/G.

SECRET

1st ARMY General STAFF.
No: G.S 73 (a)
Date: 13-4-15

G.O.C. 2nd London Div

GENERAL STAFF 2ND LONDON DIVISION
No. C/76/3
13 APR 1915
TERRITORIAL FORCE

13

Corps
Divisions
Brigades
──────────

1. The instructions contained in 1st Army Secret Memorandum dated 2nd April are cancelled so far as the operations
therein referred to are concerned. The general principles
referred to are embodied in the attached instructions –
PAPER 'B'.

2. The operations for which preparation is now being
made are intended to be much more sustained, and it is
[hoped will lead to] more far reaching results than
at NEUVE CHAPELLE.

[...] te with a vigorous offensive
[...] scale by the French with a
[...] front for a considerable width
[...] action as will cause a general
[...] the enemy's line.

[...] re, not a local success and
[...] or even a portion of the
[...] less extended front, but to
[...] disposal and fight a decisive

[...] for the attack are attached –
[...] be worked out by Corps and
[...] me lines as those for the
[...] will be submitted to Head-
[...] ly date.

[...] acking troops and reserves
[...] ed, and the construction of
[...] s and screened approaches put
[...] all the troops necessary for
[...] ssible.

[...] sed in detail beforehand in the
[...] to get into and out of their

[...] will be proceeded with without
[...] ally so as not to disclose the
[...] ted.

[...] the following papers issued

[...] 7th German Corps.
[...] E and the present German line,
[...] during the next few days.]

R. Butler.
Brigadier-General
General Staff, 1st Army.

13th April, 1915.

SECRET   1st Corps 289 G

2nd London Div

The attached copies
of 1st Army Secret instructions
are forwarded in continuation
of 1st Corps Secret Memo
No. 289 G to which they
have reference.

R Whigham
VI Corps
13/4/15

SECRET

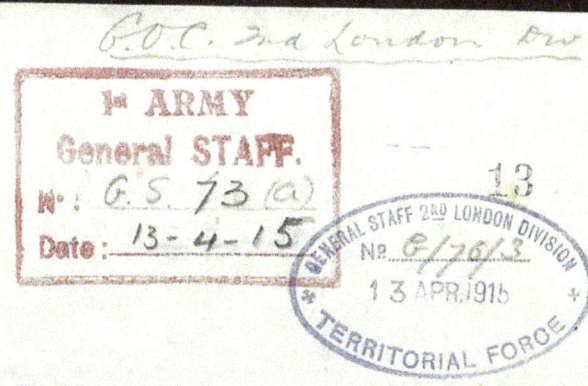

1st ARMY
General STAFF.
N°: G.S. 73 (a)
Date: 13-4-15

Corps
Divisions
Brigades

1. The instructions contained in 1st Army Secret Memorandum dated 2nd April are cancelled so far as the operations therein referred to are concerned. The general principles referred to are embodied in the attached instructions — PAPER 'B'.

2. The operations for which preparation is now being made are intended to be much more sustained, and it is hoped that they will lead to more far reaching results than could be expected from those at NEUVE CHAPELLE.

   The object is to co-operate with a vigorous offensive which is to be made on a large scale by the French with a view to breaking the enemy's front for a considerable width and then to follow up by such action as will cause a general retirement of a great part of the enemy's line.

   Our objective is, therefore, not a local success and the capture of a few trenches or even a portion of the hostile position on a more or less extended front, but to employ the entire force at our disposal and fight a decisive battle.

3. The general instructions for the attack are attached — PAPER 'A'. All details will be worked out by Corps and Divisions concerned on the same lines as those for the attack on NEUVE CHAPELLE, and will be submitted to Headquarters, 1st Army, at an early date.

4. Forming up places for attacking troops and reserves must be carefully reconnoitred, and the construction of lines of breastworks, trenches and screened approaches put in hand at once, so as to get all the troops necessary for the attack up as close as possible.

   All troops will be rehearsed in detail beforehand in the actual way in which they are to get into and out of their forming up places.

5. Registration of targets will be proceeded with without delay, and carried out gradually so as not to disclose the fact that an attack is projected.

6. Attention is directed to the following papers issued by 1st Army Intelligence :—

   (1). Area occupied by the 7th German Corps.
   (2). Country between LILLE and the present German line, (which will be issued during the next few days.)

   R. Butler.
   Brigadier-General
   General Staff, 1st Army.

13th April, 1915.

PAPER 'A'.

GENERAL INSTRUCTIONS FOR THE ATTACK.

1. The 1st Army will operate so as to break through the enemy's line and gain the LA BASSEE - LILLE road between LA BASSEE and FOURNES and then advance on DON.

2. (a). The 1st Corps, maintaining its right at GIVENCHY, will attack from its breastworks in the vicinity of RICHEBOURG L'AVOUE on as broad a front as possible and advance on RUE DE MARAIS - ILLIES.

   (b). The Indian Corps will operate so as to cover the left of the 1st Corps and will capture the FERME DU BIEZ. Its subsequent advance will be directed on LIGNY-LE-GRAND - LA CLIQUETERIE FARM.

   (c). The 4th Corps will operate so as to break through the enemy's line in the vicinity of ROUGES BANCS with the object of :-

   (1). Organizing a defensive flank from the vicinity of LA CORDONNERIE FARM to FROMELLES, and

   (2). Turning the AUBERS defences by an attack from the N.E.

   The subsequent advance will be directed on LA CLIQUETERIE FARM, with a view to effecting a junction with the Indian Corps.

3. The 2nd Cavalry Division will remain near ESTAIRES in readiness to act as the situation develops.

PAPER "B".

GENERAL PRINCIPLES FOR THE ATTACK.

1. The enemy is to be beaten on a certain length of front and driven out of it, and must not be allowed time to reform in rear of the captured trenches.
For this a <u>violent</u> and <u>continuous</u> action is required.
The keynote of all the work, both as regards details and the general idea, is offensive action.
When once the enemy's front system of trenches is broken, delay is usually the chief cause of failure and heavy casualties.
Commanders must, however, bear in mind that, once the enemy's line is broken, it is the intention to follow up by such action as will cause a general retirement of a great part of the enemy's line. Thus the operations will be continued during a considerable period.

Supports and reserves.

2. Bearing the above in mind, it is of the highest importance that all commanders should consider carefully the handling of their reserves to maintain the forward movement.
Under the existing conditions, only one definite offensive blow can be expected from one body of infantry, and, therefore, fresh troops must be pushed through those making the first attack to develop the success won. Troops heavily engaged during the day should not ordinarily be expected to continue the offensive on the following day, but should be either actually relieved or arrangements made for fresh troops to pass through them. The organization of reserves in depth should be made with this object.
Supporting and reserve troops must be close up from the commencement of the operations, so that they can follow close on the heels of the troops in front. Commanders of such troops must clearly understand the objective and their role, and use their initiative.
Ample cover must be provided for the reserve troops well forward, with good and sufficient communicating trenches. Direction boards must be put up to prevent mistakes in the existing labyrinth of trenches.

The Infantry attack.

3. Infantry commanders must know the time table of artillery fire, and regulate their progress and time their assaults in accordance with it.
The attack on the front trenches will probably not be equally successful all along the line. Support must be given at once to the units which have been successful to enable them to press on. Where unsuccessful a new attack must be organized from a flank where the line has been broken.
If a certain body of infantry fails to gain its own particular local objective, there is no reason why the troops on either flank should be held up. Every body of infantry must push on and thereby facilitate the task of the troops on the right and left.
The whole operation can be regulated with the greatest precision. Parties of infantry should be detailed beforehand for the capture of the several localities at definitely stated times in accordance with the artillery time table. The accuracy of photographic maps permits of this being done.

We must not wait to be counter attacked, but must follow up our attack at once. Infantry must push on, and field guns, trench mortars, machine guns, etc., must be pushed forward in close support of the attacking infantry to batter down houses, etc., The responsibility for supporting the attacking infantry in this way rests with Infantry Commanders, and special guns will be allotted to them for this purpose.

Localities must be seized promptly to act as supporting points to further advance, but only the necessary number of men will be left to entrench each of these points.

All ground gained will be secured (F.S.R. Part I, Sec. 105 (5)).

Artillery

4. The artillery objective is not only the wire entanglements and front trenches, but the whole position, with a view to destroying the hostile infantry, actually and morally. (i.e. second line, communication trenches, shelters, etc., must be systematically dealt with.)

The task of the artillery is :-
(a). The support of the infantry during its attack.
(b). To gain superiority of fire over the hostile artillery.

The artillery fire will be time-tabled and registered as far behind the enemy's front line trenches as possible, with due regard to range and accuracy.

The guns must be registered beforehand on all the objectives and tactical localities as far forward as possible.

Similarly, the barrages of shrapnel must be arranged beforehand. These will be gradually expanded as the infantry advances.

The nature of the artillery support required by the infantry depends on the local conditions of the fight.

Some field or horse artillery guns must be ready to push forward rapidly in support of the infantry as the latter get beyond the support of the remaining guns.(Field Artillery Training, Sec. 156 (4).)

Special Parties

5. Special parties must be detailed for work subsidiary to the attack, such as bomb parties, sandbag parties, bayonet parties, entrenching tool parties. These parties must all be conversant with their various duties.

The idea of the offensive must be inculcated in the grenadier parties, so that their efforts are directed to bombing so as to assist the movement to front and flank, rather than to more defensive work and blocking approaches.

Special attention must be given to repairing roads and detachments of R.E., with infantry working parties attached, must be organized and in position to follow up the attack, for clearing away obstacles and mending roads, to allow free passage for troops.

Special parties for extending and maintaining the telephone wires must also be organized beforehand (see paragraph 7).

R.E. Stores & Materials.

6. Advanced depots of R.E. stores must be established close up behind our own lines at short intervals along the front of the attack. These depots should contain material for entanglements, sandbags, trench-bridging materials, tools, etc.,

Parties of R.E. with infantry must be specially detailed to move forward with these stores to secure positions gained.

The experience of NEUVE CHAPELLE gives a good indication of the nature and quantities of stores required for any given length of line, and estimates should be framed accordingly with regard to the length of the probable successive lines likely to be required to be placed in a state of defence.

Communications.

7. In order that the offensive may be continued without interruption and be suited to the changing conditions of the fight, the several commanders must be kept in close touch with the situation: hence communications must be carefully organized beforehand and adequate means of getting information back from the front provided. Wherever possible communications should be triplicated and arrangements made to carry on communications by flags, lamps, etc., when wires are broken. <u>This is of the first importance, and all commanders will give this matter their close attention.</u>

The ground over which the attack is to pass and the localities to be attacked can in most cases be seen and studied. So far as is possible, therefore, arrangements should be made beforehand between what points communication by flag or otherwise is to be established as the attack progresses.

The positions of commanders must be carefully thought out and suitably protected points organized for commanders near their troops.

Telegraph and telephone wires must be buried up to our front trenches, and arrangements made to push wires on as soon as possible after the attack has passed beyond them.

Staff officers must be pushed well forward with the object of collecting information and keeping commanders regularly informed of the situation.

With this object in view, positions of observation and dugouts should be made, and special communications established beforehand with these places.

Special attention must be given to instructing signal companies in their duties and action during an advance, and all preparations must be made with a view to the forward movement being sustained.

Divisional Cavalry and Cyclists.

8. Divisional Cavalry and Cyclists must be kept handy to push on rapidly as opportunity offers, to anticipate the enemy in occupying houses and other tactical points, and so facilitating the advance after the enemy's main lines of defence have been broken.

2nd London Division.

INSTRUCTION OF TERRITORIAL BATTALIONS.

18th and 20th London Battalions (attached 6th Brigade.)

    20th London have one company attached to A.1.
    18th London take over A.2 and CUINCHY Supporting Point this afternoon.

17th and 19th London Battns. (attached 5th Brigade).

    1 Coy, 19th London took up line allotted to 1 company in C.1.
    1 Coy, 17th ,, ,, ,, ,, ,, ,, 1 company in C.2.
    Each battalion provided two reliefs each of 100 men for working parties.

15th London Battalion (attached 4th Brigade).

    In the trenches tonight, (B.)

[signature]
                      Major-General,
13th April, 1915.   Commanding 2nd Division.

2.

Fourth
Fifth Lon. Inf. Bdes.

        For information and retention

                              Major,
                           General Staff,
14th April 1915.   Second Lon. Div.
2 L.D. No. 2/8/G.

2nd London Division.

INSTRUCTION OF TERRITORIAL BATTALIONS.

18th & 20th London Battalions (attached 6th Brigade.)
20th London relieve 18th London in A 2. and CUINCHY support point.

17th & 19th London Battalions (attached 5th Brigade.)
As yesterday.

15th London Battalion. (attached 4th Brigade.)
In B.1. and doing well.

                                                      Major-General,

14th April, 1915.   Commanding 2nd Division.

CONFIDENTIAL.

2nd Division.

REPORT ON 15TH CIVIL SERVICE.

This battalion did 4 days by platoons in trenches and 2 days as a whole battalion in B.1.

I consider them quite satisfactory with exception of one small point :-

I did not think the officers employed with <u>working parties</u> took enough interest in the work in hand, but were inclined to wait about headquarters till it was done, instead of guiding and superintending.

The reports sent in were clear and concise and the men showed great keenness in the trenches.

(sd) CAVAN, Brigadier-General,
16th April, 1915.   Commanding 4th (Guards) Brigade.

2nd Division.

Report on 17th London Territorial Battalion.

Their work in the breastworks was satisfactory and they kept a good look out. They are however inclined to rely on looking through loopholes at night instead of over the parapet. They were steady under fire, though no severe strain was imposed. They should be fit to take their place in the front line, but further work alongside regulars would be desirable.

Sanitation in the front line requires attention. They are inclined to foul the ground in the vicinity of the breastworks.

They were keen and soldierlike and their work in working parties was quite satisfactory.

Report on 19th London Territorial Battalion.

Remarks above apply equally to this battalion.

It is important that they should be instructed to trust to their ears more than they appear to do at night.

(sd) A.A.CHICHESTER, Bdr-Genl,
16th April, 1915.   Comdg., 5th Inf.Brigade.

2nd London Division.

INSTRUCTION OF TERRITORIAL BATTALIONS.
****

18th & 20th Battalions (attached 6th Brigade.)

 Instruction completed - assembling in BETHUNE.
 Each battalion has held part of line under its own regimental staff.

17th & 19th Battalions.(attached 5th Brigade.).

 Instruction as yesterday - now completed.

15th London Battalion. (attached 4th Brigade.)

 Completed.

            H. S. Horne

            Major-General,
15th April, 1915. Commanding 2nd Division.

     2.

Fourth
Fifth Lon. Inf. Bdes.

  For information and retention.

         Major,
        General Staff,
16th April 1915. Second Lon. Div.
2 L.D.No. 2/8/G.

Suggested plan for Move of Battalions of 2nd London
Division to 2nd Division Area, 18th and 19th April.
―――――――――

"A" Section.   (5th Infantry Brigade.)
       Battalions affiliated :- 6th and 7th London.

   On Sunday 18th :-   6th London Battalion marches to
                        BETHUNE. Its C.O. and Company
                        Commanders report to 5th Brigade
                        Headquarters at 5 p.m.

   On morning 19th:-   6th London Battalion marches from
                        BETHUNE to trenches in A.3 under orders
                        of G.O.C., 5th Infantry Brigade.
                        7th London Battalion marches to BETHUNE.
                        ――――――――――

"B" Section.   (4th (Guards) Brigade.)
       Battalions affiliated:- 9th and 18th London.

   On Sunday 18th :-   Officers of 18th London Battalion
                        report to 4th Brigade Headquarters at
                        2.30 p.m. to go over the trenches.

   On Monday 19th :-   18th London Battalion moves by towpath
                        from BETHUNE to trenches under orders
                        of G.O.C., 4th (Guards) Brigade.
                        9th London Battalion marches to LE
                        PREOL, from its present billets, leaving
                        BETHUNE at 2.30 p.m. and following the
                        towpath thence.
                        ――――――――――

"C" Section.   (6th Infantry Brigade.)
       Battalions affiliated :- 17th, 18th, 19th and 20th
                                 London Battalions.

   On Sunday 18th :-   C.O., 17th London Battalion reports at
                        6th Brigade Headquarters at 2.30 p.m.

   On Sunday 19th :-   17th London Battalion marches from
                        BETHUNE to trenches under orders of G.O.C.
                        6th Infantry Brigade.
                        18th London Battalion marches from
                        BETHUNE to GORRE during afternoon.
                        19th London Battalion marches from
                        present billets to LA BEUVRIERE.
                        20th London Battalion marches from
                        present billets to LAPUGNOY.
                        ――――――――――

                        Forwarded for information and necessary action.

2.L.D. 97/2   C.B. Bannen   Lieut Colonel,
17th April, 1915.   General Staff,
                                        2nd London Division.

1st Guards Brigade.

       Report on the training of "A" company 23rd Battalion
                The London Regiment.

      "A" Company, 23rd Battalion London Regiment, was attached to my battalion April 11th to April 15th, 1915. A platoon was attached to each company for duty in the trenches.

      From reports received from O=C., companies under my command, and from my own personal observation, I consider they carried out their duties in a very satisfactory manner. I was of opinion that the officers and N.C.Os of this "A" Company, 23rd Battalion The London Regiment, require to take more personal supervision and should not, especially when attached to a regular battalion, be afraid of asking questions or enquiring how duties should be carried out. They appeared to be rather diffident on this matter. The men were in very good spirits and very keen. They were employed also as working parties and carried out these duties quietly and well. Their sentries were acquainted with their orders, but require to be constantly on the alert.

      I consider that they are now fully qualified to take up their duties as a company on its own in the trenches.

18th April, 1915.   (Sd) J.Ponsonby, Lieut-Colonel,
                        Comdg: 1st Bn: Coldstream Guards.

1st Guards Brigade.
- - - - -

B.W. 67. 20.4.1915.

Report on "B" Company, 23rd Battalion, The London Regt: attached 1/The Black Watch, for instruction from 11th April to 15th April, 1915.

Captain Wilkins, commanding the company, appeared to me to be especially capable. Of the other officers, Lieut: Radcliffe struck me as a good platoon leader, while Captain Van Neck, Lieuts: Berry and Van Neck were all extremely keen and hardworking. The sergeant commanding 1 platoon was satisfactory. The N.C.Os generally need to learn that they must give orders, not instructions, to those under them.

All the officers seem to deal directly with privates too much and not work sufficiently through the N.C.Os. The N.C.Os. must be made to accept responsibility if they are ever to be trained to be of real use.

The men during the four days showed themselves good, willing workers - keen, intelligent, and in the best of spirits

My four days experience of the company conveyed the impression that it was both efficient and well trained and fit to take its place in the firing line.

(Sd) C.E.Stewart, Lieut-Colonel,
Comdg: 1st The Black Watch.

CONFIDENTIAL.   6th Bde.No. 495.

H.Q., 2nd Division.

        The 18th and 20th London Regiments have during their tour of duty in this Brigade been employed as follows :-

For each Battn. 1. <u>Trench Duties.</u> The whole battalion was gradually put through 24 hours of individual instruction in the trenches, 2 platoons at a time being put in the front line and each man going on duty alongside a regular soldier. Remaining 2 platoons of a company being in support and employed on such duties as trench repairs, etc. After 24 hours, the half companies changed round and at the end of eight days every platoon had undergone a tour of duty, both in the front line and support.

        In addition at the close of the period of attachment the battalion was given a particular portion of the line to hold with two companies for 24 hours under its own regimental staff.

        The men worked well and were very keen and no fault was to be found with the vigilance of the sentries at night but the officers and N.C.O's seemed hardly yet to have realized the responsibilities of their position when in the front line and the necessity of maintaining constant command over their men at all times. Orders are often correctly given but the necessary supervision in seeing that they are carried out is apt to be neglected.

2.   A good deal of experience was gained in digging trenches under R.E. supervision. The men worked hard but do not as yet work as quickly as regulars.

3.   All ranks were always keen and willing.

        During their attachment they were fairly well initiated into an experience of gun and rifle fire and suffered a few casualties.

                                                                 Each

Each battalion should with assistance and supervision be able to hold an easy section of the line with regular troops on their right and left.

                                              (Sd) C.J. STEAMENSON. Lieut.Colonel.

17/4/15.   Commanding 6th Infy. Brigade.

2/London Div 76/5

SECRET. 1st Corps No. 289 (G).

~~1st Division.~~
~~2nd Division.~~
2nd London Division.
----

1. The attached copy of 1st Corps Draft Operation Order is forwarded in substitution for the "Instructions" forwarded to you on the 17th instant, which are to be destroyed.

2. The G.O.C. will hold a conference at BETHUNE at 10 a.m. on Tuesday, 20th. The following will attend :-

    G.Os.C., G.S.Os. 1st Grade, and C.R.As. of
        1st, 2nd, and 2nd London Divisions.

G.O.C. 2nd Division will please arrange for a suitable room for this conference.

3. A draft of the 1st and 2nd Division Operation Order, with a covering minute explaining the arrangements for forming up, establishment of R.E. Depots, ammunition and food supply, and other essential details will be forwarded in duplicate to 1st Corps Headquarters (marked "Secret") by 10 a.m. Wednesday, 21st, for transmission to 1st Army.

                                        R. Whigham Brig. General.
18th April, 1915.   General Staff, 1st Corps.

S E C R E T.   Copy No. 3

1st CORPS DRAFT OPERATION ORDER.

1915.

1. The task of the 1st Corps is to break the enemy's line opposite RICHEBOURG l'AVOUE and advance on ILLIES, maintaining its right at GIVENCHY.

2. The Indian Corps will attack on the left of the 1st Corps with the CROSS-ROADS at LA TOURELLE, the DISTILLERY just SOUTH of those CROSS-ROADS, and the FERME DU BIEZ as its first objectives. Its subsequent advance will be directed on LIGNY LE PETIT - LIGNY LE GRAND - LA CLIQUETERIE FARM.

3. To carry out the task of the 1st Corps the 1st Division will attack from its breastworks in front of RICHEBOURG l'AVOUE on a front of two brigades. Its first objective will be THE ORCHARD.(S.21.c.), LA QUINQUE RUE, and the road joining LA QUINQUE RUE and LA TOURELLE. From this line the advance will be directed on RUE DU MARAIS - LORGIES - ILLIES.

4. The remainder of the 1st Corps front, namely from CUINCHY and CUINCHY to the ROAD JUNCTION, S.14.b. (exclusive) will be held by the 4th Guards Brigade (GIVENCHY) and two brigades 2nd London Division. These three brigades will be under command of G.O.C. 2nd London Division.

5. The 2nd Division (less 4th Guards Brigade), with one brigade 2nd London Division attached, 1 section No. 7 Mountain Battery, and the Motor Machine Gun Battery, will form the 1st Corps Reserve, and will be assembled in readiness in the area LOISNE - LE TOURET - LES FACONS - LE HAMEL.

6. The attack of the 1st Division will be supported by No. 1 Group H.A.R., and in addition to the 1st Divisional Artillery the following guns will be at the disposal of G.O.C. 1st Division :-

       1st Siege Battery.
       4th Siege Battery.
       2 Siege Batteries from 1st Group H.A.R.
       60th Battery, R.F.A. (Hows).
       47th Battery, R.F.A. (Hows) (to be located approximately
           in its present position west of FESTUBERT).
       1 Section 56th Battery, R.F.A. (Hows).
       8th London Brigade, R.F.A. (Hows).
       4th West Riding Brigade, R.F.A. (Hows).
       35th Heavy Battery, R.G.A.
       2 sections No 7 Mountain Battery.
       2 Trench Mortar Batteries.
       "N", "V" & "X" Batteries, R.H.A.
       2 Armoured Motor Cars with 3 pr. Q.F. guns.
       1 Brigade, R.F.A., 2nd Divnl. Artillery.
       1 Brigade, R.F.A., 2nd London Divnl. Artillery.

7. Arrangements are to be made so that trench mortars, and mountain, horse and field guns can be pushed forward in close support of the infantry as it advances.

8. The following artillery will be at disposal of the G.O.C. 2nd London Division to support the defensive front referred to in para. 4:-
       2nd London Divnl. Artillery (less 1 brigade 15 prs. and
                                    8th London Brigade (Hows).
       1 brigade, R.F.A., 2nd Division.
       56th Battery, R.F.A., less 1 section.
       26th Heavy Battery, R.G.A.
   The G.O.C. 2nd London Division may call on the 47th Battery, R.F.A. (Hows) in case of emergency.

9. The 1st Bn. Queen's Regiment will be assembled in readiness at ROAD JUNCTION W.30.c. directly under the orders of the Corps Commander.

10. The artillery bombardment will begin at 0.00 a.m. and will be carried out in accordance to time table (Appendix   ). At   a.m. the assault by the infantry of the 1st Division will be carried out.

11. At 0.00 a.m. the 15 pr. and 18 pr. batteries with the 2nd London Division will open fire on portions of the enemy's wire entanglements in front of CUINCHY, GIVENCHY and FESTUBERT which have been previously registered. Simultaneously with this, bursts of rifle and machine gun fire will be opened and maintained on the hostile trenches all along the 1st Corps front.

12. "Advanced 1st Corps" will be established at BETHUNE at   on

2nd London Division to attack in direction of Rue d'Ouvert and press on towards Violaines + BRAU POITS.

London Div/76/5A 8
G.S.O.1, 2nd Lon. Divn.

SECRET.   Notes for 1st Corps Conference.

                              20th April 1915.

1. Forming up places, with suitable communication trenches to and from them, are of special importance. Copies of a diagram shewing a type used by the French have been issued to Divisions.
   2nd Division is responsible for the provision of forming up places for its own use about RUE de L'EPINETTE and INDIAN VILLAGE.

2. Troops must go through a regular rehearsal of the method of getting into and out of the trenches from which they will assault.

3. R.E.Store Depots, location of, for use of all Divisions.

4. Batteries not now in position must be moved into position under cover of darkness. All such movements must be completed in time to admit of proper registration.

5. Reserves of S.A.A. must be arranged in front line trenches from which the assault is to be made. Each man will start with as many rounds as he can conveniently carry, but in no case less than 200.

6. Each man will start with his "iron ration" complete; 1st line Cookers and supply section of train will both be full on morning fixed for assault. Arrangements must be made to get food forward at nightfall.

7. C.E., 1st Corps, is having wooden tramway manufactured. Two lines of this should be laid as the situation permits, say one line from CHOCOLAT MENIER and the other from INDIAN VILLAGE.

8. What arrangements can be made to get forward great coats and kits left behind.

9. Every man carry a sandbag.

10. Distinguishing flags and other devices to shew position of attacking infantry.

11. Multiplication of means of inter-communication; burying cables; use of lamp signalling by day.

12. Avoid committing too many men to the assault all at once. If the Artillery does its work the assault on the first line of hostile trenches should easily succeed.

13. Machine guns; will some of them be brigaded ?

14. Divisional Mounted Troops and Cyclists. Where will they be posted in readiness and what will be their role when the hostile line is broken.

15. R.E.parties to bridge hostile trenches and open up communication.

16. Maps shewing areas of concentration and traffic circuits will be issued to all Divisions (Secret)

Notes
London Div. Conference 21.4.15

GOC, 3/s, AQMG, CRA, CRE, ADMS, OC Train
Signals — Inf Brigadiers

4" fds Signal Sect —
CRA billets —

Rue du Bois

SECRET.   Copy No. 3

1st CORPS OPERATION ORDER No. 77.

20th April, 1915.

1. The London Division will relieve the infantry of the 2nd Division (less 4th Guards Brigade), and that of the 1st Division south of CHOCOLAT MENIER CORNER, on 24th and 25th April. The relief will be carried out under inter-divisional arrangements so as to be completed by 10 a.m. 25th April, at which hour G.O.C. London Division will assume command of the front CUINCHY - CHOCOLAT MENIER CORNER.

2. The artillery at disposal of G.O.C. London Division will be as stated in para. 7, 1st Corps Secret Instructions, 289 (G) of 20th April. The F.A. Brigade (15 prs.) of the London Division located near RUE DE l'EPINETTE, and the 47th Howitzer Battery will be at disposal of London Division until required to support the attack of the 1st Division.

3. The necessary artillery reliefs will be carried out after the infantry reliefs and, as far as possible, under cover of darkness, and will be completed by 6 a.m. 27th April.

4. Daily progress of the reliefs to be reported to 1st Corps.

R. Whigham Brig. General.
General Staff, 1st Corps.

Issued at 7 p.m. to :-

    1st Division.
    2nd Division.
    London Division.
    Indian Corps.

SECRET.   Copy No. 3

1st CORPS INSTRUCTIONS.

Reference maps (1/40,000, Sheet BETHUNE.
(1/20,000, B Series, Sheet 36 S.W.
(1/10,000

289 (G). 20th April, 1915.

1. In accordance with the instructions contained in 1st Army Secret Memorandum G.S.73(a), dated 13th April, copies of which have been issued to divisions, the task of the 1st Corps is to break the enemy's line opposite RICHEBOURG l'AVOUE and advance on ILLIES, maintaining its right at GIVENCHY.

2. The Indian Corps will attack on the left of the 1st Corps with the CROSS-ROADS at LA TOURELLE, the DISTILLERY just SOUTH of those CROSS-ROADS and the FERME DU BIEZ as its first objectives. Its subsequent advance will be directed on LIGNY LE PETIT - LIGNY LE GRAND - LA CLIQUETERIE FARM.

3. To carry out the task of the 1st Corps the 1st Division will attack from its breastworks in front of RICHEBOURG l'AVOUE on a front of two brigades. Its first objectives will be the hostile trenches P.8. and P.10, the FARM COUR d'AVOUE, and the road running from that farm to LA TOURELLE. From this line the advance will be directed on RUE DU MARAIS - LORGIES - ILLIES.

4. The remainder of the 1st Corps front, namely from CUINCHY to CHOCOLAT MENIER CORNER, S.14.b. (exclusive) will be held by the 4th Guards Brigade (CUINCHY and GIVENCHY) and two brigades London Division. These three brigades will be under command of G.O.C. London Division.

5. The 2nd Division (less 4th Guards Brigade), with one brigade London Division attached, 1 section No. 7 Mountain Battery, and the Motor Machine Gun Battery, will form the 1st Corps Reserve, and will be assembled in readiness in the area LOISNE - LE TOURET - LES CHOQUAUX - ESSARS.

6. The attack of the 1st Division will be supported by No. 1 Group H.A.R., and in addition to the 1st Divisional Artillery the following guns will be at the disposal of the G.O.C. 1st Division :-

        1st Siege Battery.
        4th Siege Battery.
        2 Siege Batteries from 1st Group H.A.R.
        60th Battery, R.F.A. (Hows).
        47th Battery, R.F.A. (Hows) (to be located approximately
            in its present position west of FESTUBERT).
        1 Section 56th Battery, R.F.A. (Hows).
        4th West Riding Brigade, R.F.A. (Hows).
        8th London Brigade, R.F.A. (Hows).
        35th Heavy Battery, R.G.A.
        2 sections No. 7 Mountain Battery.
        2 Trench Mortar Batteries.
        "N", "V" & "X" Batteries, R.H.A.
        2 Armoured Motor Cars with 3 pr.Q.F. guns.
        1 Brigade, R.F.A., 2nd Divnl. Artillery.
        1 Brigade, R.F.A., London Divnl. Artillery, (to be
            located about the RUE DE l'EPINETTE and LE TOURET).

Arrangements are to be made so that trench mortars, and mountain, horse and field guns can be pushed forward in close support of the infantry as it advances.

7. The following artillery will be at disposal of the G.O.C. London Division to support the defensive front referred to in para. 4 :-

    London Divnl. Artillery (less 1 brigade (15 prs.) and 8th London Brigade (Hows)).
    1 Brigade, R.F.A. (18 prs.), 2nd Division.
    56th Battery, R.F.A., less 1 section.
    26th Heavy Battery, R.G.A.

The G.O.C. London Division may call on the 47th Battery, R.F.A. (Hows) in case of emergency.

8. The 1st Bn. Queen's Regiment will be assembled in readiness west of ROAD JUNCTION W.30.c. directly under the orders of the Corps Commander.

                                            R. Whigham Brig. General.
                                                General Staff, 1st Corps.

Issued at 7 p.m. to :-

    1st Division.
    2nd Division.
    London Division.
    Indian Corps.

CONFIDENTIAL.

1st Brigade.

From 11th to 15th April each company of this battalion had a platoon of "C" Company of the 23rd Battalion, The London Regiment, attached to it as 5th platoon. On the night of the 15th they were attached to the Gloucester Regt: instead.

Captain A.T.Fearon showed great keenness and looked well after his men.

Captain R.S.M.Grindel appeared to know his work, but would do better of he realised the necessity of seeing personally that his orders are carried out.

2/Lieut: A.P.Clarke is keen, hardworking, and likely to make a good officer.

2/Lieut: P.W.J.Stevenson is very keen and anxious to learn about trench warfare.

The N.C.Os in some cases kept good discipline and were up to their work, but there was often a lack of supervision and control, the men being left too much to their own devices.

Amongst the junior N.C.Os much talking was required to get orders carried out.

The men were intelligent, willing and of promising material. They kept their arms, equipment, and trenches clean, and did well on working parties. Sentries were inclined to gossip with the other men and the danger of the close proximity of the Germans seemed to be realized thoroughly only when hostile bullets were coming over the parapet.

On the whole the company was not quite up to that of the 21st Battalion of their regiment, but experience will rapidly increase their value.

HINGETTE. (Sd) E.Craig-Brown, Major,
21.4.1915. Comdg: 1st Cameron Highs.

SECRET.   Copy No. 3

1st CORPS OPERATION ORDER No. 78.

23rd April, 1915.

1. With reference to 1st Corps Operation Order No. 77, dated 20th April, the G.O.C. 2nd Division will retain command of the CUINCHY and GIVENCHY sections for the present.

2. G.O.C. London Division will assume command of the FESTUBERT section and the right section of the 1st Division front as far north as CHOCOLAT MENIER CORNER (exclusive) from 10 a.m. tomorrow. Headquarters London Division will be in BETHUNE. 10AM 25.

3. The 4th London Brigade will remain under the orders of the G.O.C. London Division for the present.

4. The artillery dispositions and reliefs as between 2nd Division and London Division will be effected as previously ordered.

5. The necessary adjustment of billeting areas will be carried out by mutual arrangement between 2nd Division and London Division.

                                            R.Whigham Brig. General.
                                            General Staff, 1st Corps.

Issued at 2 p.m. to :-

    1st Division.
    2nd Division.
    London Division.
    Indian Corps. - For information.
    1st Army.   -   ,,   ,,

"C" Form (Duplicate). Army Form C. 2123.
MESSAGES AND SIGNALS.

Handed in at UCB   Office

TO London Divn

Sender's Number: G749   Day of Month: 23rd

My operation order no seventy
eight para two aaa for
ten am prisoners read ten am
april twenty fifth

Ln Div/29
6-30 pm

FROM / PLACE & TIME: 1st Corps 6 pm

SECRET.   Copy No. 1

LONDON DIVISION OPERATION ORDER No.1.

(Reference - Bethune Combined Sheets, 1/40,000).

23rd April, 1915.

Intention. 1. Under instructions from 1st Corps the G.O.C. assumes command of "C" Section (FESTUBERT) and that portion of the right section of the 1st Division (D 1) as far north as CHOCOLAT MENIER CORNER (exclusive) from 10 a.m. 25th instant.

Detail. 2.(a). INFANTRY.

By 10 a.m. 25th instant the above line will be held as follows :-

"C" Section (FESTUBERT) . 5th Lon.Inf.Brigade.

"D 1" Section as far as CHOCOLAT MENIER CORNER (exclusive) . 6th Lon.Inf.Brigade.

4th Lon.Inf.Brigade will be held as Divisional Reserve at LABEUVRIERE and LAPUGNOY.

G.O's C. 5th and 6th London Infantry Brigades will take over from the 5th and 3rd Infantry Brigades respectively on the night of 24th/25th April under arrangements to be made direct between Brigade Commanders concerned.

All trench stores, including mortars, will be taken over from outgoing units.

(b). ARTILLERY.

The 5th London Brigade R.F.A. is attached to the 1st Division, but is at the disposal of the C.R.A. London Division until required to support the 1st Division.

The reliefs and dispositions as between the 2nd Division and London Division will be carried out after the Infantry reliefs are completed, under arrangements to be made direct with the G.O's C., R.A. concerned according to instructions already communicated to the G.O.C., R.A. London Division.

The reliefs will be carried out as far as possible under cover of darkness and will be completed by 6 a.m. 27th April. Daily progress of relief will be reported to Divisional Headquarters.

Infantry Brigades will be supplied with S.A.A. as follows :-
5th Lon.Inf.Bde., by 7th Lon.Bde. R.F.A.
6th Lon.Inf.Bde., by 6th Lon.Bde. R.F.A.

The 6th London Infantry Brigade can also call upon the 36th Brigade R.F.A. if required.

Positions of R.F.A. Brigade Ammunition Columns are as follows :-
36th Brigade R.F.A. . ECLUSE D'ESSARS (X.19.c).
6th Lon.Bde. R.F.A. . FERME DE ROI (E.6.c).
7th   ,,   . . Distillery BETHUNE (E.12.a).

(c).

(c). ENGINEERS.

Field Companies will be allotted as follows :-

3rd London Field Company R.E. to the 5th London Infantry Brigade.
4th London Field Company R.E. to the 6th London Infantry Brigade.
The Officers and N.C.O's of the 5th Field Company R.E. have been placed at the disposal of the C.R.E. by 2nd Division on 25th April, to show the 3rd London Field Company R.E. round "C" Section (FESTUBERT).

(d). MOVES.

The 3rd and 4th London Field Companies R.E. will move on the 24th April to the billets arranged for them by G.O's C. 5th and 6th London Infantry Brigades in conjunction with the C.R.E., at times to be ordered by the C.R.E., but not before 2 p.m.

The 4th Lon.Inf.Brigade will move to LABEUVRIERE and LAPUGNOY as directed in 2nd Division Operation Order No. 36, dated 23rd April 1915.

The 19th and 20th Battalions, London Regiment, will march from LABEUVRIERE and LAPUGNOY respectively at 1 p.m. on 24th April, via ANNEZIN, to the 5th Lon.Inf.Bde.Area.

London Division Cyclist Company will move at 1 p.m. 24th April and proceed to billets in BETHUNE.

Units moving through BETHUNE from the WEST to the 5th and 6th Lon.Inf.Brigade Areas will proceed by RUE D'AIRE - RUE DU PONT NEUF - RUE DU PONT DE PIERRES - road junction W.30.c.

(e). BILLETS.

Artillery. Wagon lines and R.F.A. Brigade Ammunition
Columns will be billeted as arranged by the G.O.C.R.A.

Infantry Brigades.
5th Lon.Inf.Bde. is allotted all billeting accommodation available in the area MARAIS - LE CROIX DE FER - LA MOTTE - RUE DE BETHUNE.

The allotment to the 6th Lon.Inf.Bde. will be issued later.

(f). CONTROL POSTS.

Control posts and Guards west of the allotted front and north of the Canal, now maintained by the 2nd Division, will be taken over by 3 p.m. 24th April as follows :-
ECLUSE D'ESSARS   -   X.19.a.
HALTE.   .   -   W.24.c.
HALTE.   .   -   W.30.c.
Instructions have already been issued to all concerned with reference to these.

Medical. 3. The 4th London Field Ambulance will remain at RAIMBERT, and the 5th London Field Ambulance at ALLOUAGNE, until further orders.

The 6th London Field Ambulance will march on 26th April, at 8 a.m., to BETHUNE, and will billet and open at ECOLE MICHELET.

The Bearer Division of this unit will take over the existing Advanced Dressing Station at TUNING FORK (F.5.a) from 2nd Division, and will open a new Advanced Dressing Station at LE TOURET (X.16.d) by 10 a.m. 25th April, and will evacuate to the 5th Field Ambulance until the 6th London Field Ambulance has opened.

This unit will be responsible for clearing the area occupied by the 5th and 6th London Infantry Brigades.

The Divisional Sanitary Section will march to BETHUNE on 24th April at 1 p.m.

The Motor Ambulance Workshop unit will remain at LAPUGNOY until arrangements are completed for its move to BETHUNE.

Supply. 4. Supply Refilling Point will be at BETHUNE.

Reports. 5. Divisional Report Centre will close at MENSECQ at 2 p.m. 24th April, and will re-open at building now occupied by the 2nd Division Signals (Marche aux Poulets, BETHUNE) at the same hour.

Wm Thwaites
Lt.Colonel,
General Staff,
London Division.

Issued at 10 p.m. :-

Copy No. 1. Operation Order File.
 ,,   2.   ,,
 ,,   3.   ,,
 ,,   4.   ,,
 ,,   5. A.A.&.Q.M.G.
 ,,   6. 5th Lon.Inf.Brigade.
 ,,   7. 6th Lon.Inf.Brigade.
 ,,   8. G.O.C.,R.A.
 ,,   9. C.R.E.
 ,,   10. London Cyclist Company.
 ,,   11. London Signal Company.
 ,,   12. A.D.M.S.
 ,,   13. O.C. London Train.
 ,,   14. A.P.M.
 ,,   15. Town Commandant, BETHUNE.
 ,,   16. 1st Corps.
 ,,   17. 1st Division.
 ,,   18. 2nd Division.
 ,,   19. 4th Lon.Inf.Bde.

S E C R E T.

Copy No. 2

LONDON DIVISION OPERATION ORDER No.1.

(Reference - Bethune Combined Sheets, 1/40,000).

23rd April, 1915.

Intention. 1. Under instructions from 1st Corps the G.O.C. assumes command of "C" Section (FESTUBERT) and that portion of the right section of the 1st Division (D 1) as far north as CHOCOLAT MENIER CORNER (exclusive) from 10 a.m. 25th instant.

Detail. 2.(a). INFANTRY.

By 10 a.m. 25th instant the above line will be held as follows :-

"C" Section (FESTUBERT) . 5th Lon.Inf.Brigade.

"D 1" Section as far as CHOCOLAT
MENIER CORNER (exclusive) . 6th Lon.Inf.Brigade.

4th Lon.Inf.Brigade will be held as Divisional Reserve at LABEUVRIERE and LAPUGNOY.

G.O's C. 5th and 6th London Infantry Brigades will take over from the 5th and 3rd Infantry Brigades respectively on the night of 24th/25th April under arrangements to be made direct between Brigade Commanders concerned.

All trench stores, including mortars, will be taken over from outgoing units.

(b). ARTILLERY.

The 5th London Brigade R.F.A. is attached to the 1st Division, but is at the disposal of the C.R.A. London Division until required to support the 1st Division.

The reliefs and dispositions as between the 2nd Division and London Division will be carried out after the Infantry reliefs are completed, under arrangements to be made direct with the G.O's C., R.A. concerned according to instructions already communicated to the G.O.C., R.A. London Division.

The reliefs will be carried out as far as possible under cover of darkness and will be completed by 6 a.m. 27th April. Daily progress of relief will be reported to Divisional Headquarters.

Infantry Brigades will be supplied with S.A.A. as follows :-

5th Lon.Inf.Bde., by 7th Lon.Bde. R.F.A.
6th Lon.Inf.Bde., by 6th Lon.Bde. R.F.A.

The 6th London Infantry Brigade can also call upon the 36th Brigade R.F.A. if required.

Positions of R.F.A. Brigade Ammunition Columns are as follows :-

36th Brigade R.F.A. . ECLUSE D'ESSARS (X.19.c).
6th Lon.Bde. R.F.A. . FERME DE ROI (E.6.c).
7th ,, . . Distillery BETHUNE (E.12.a).

(c).

(c). ENGINEERS.

Field Companies will be allotted as follows :-

3rd London Field Company R.E. to the 5th London Infantry Brigade.

4th London Field Company R.E. to the 6th London Infantry Brigade.

The Officers and N.C.O's of the 5th Field Company R.E. have been placed at the disposal of the C.R.E. by 2nd Division on 25th April, to show the 3rd London Field Company R.E. round "C" Section (FESTUBERT).

(d). MOVES.

The 3rd and 4th London Field Companies R.E. will move on the 24th April to the billets arranged for them by G.O's C. 5th and 6th London Infantry Brigades in conjunction with the C.R.E., at times to be ordered by the C.R.E., but not before 2 p.m.

The 4th Lon.Inf.Brigade will move to LABEUVRIERE and LAPUGNOY as directed in 2nd Division Operation Order No. 36, dated 23rd April 1915.

The 19th and 20th Battalions, London Regiment, will march from LABEUVRIERE and LAPUGNOY respectively at 1 p.m. on 24th April, via ANNEZIN, to the 5th Lon.Inf.Bde.Area.

London Division Cyclist Company will move at 1 p.m. 24th April and proceed to billets in BETHUNE.

Units moving through BETHUNE from the WEST to the 5th and 6th Lon.Inf.Brigade Areas will proceed by RUE D'AIRE - RUE DU PONT NEUF - RUE DU PONT DE PIERRES - road junction W.30.c.

(e). BILLETS.

Artillery. Wagon lines and R.F.A. Brigade Ammunition Columns will be billeted as arranged by the G.O.C.R.A.

Infantry Brigades.
5th Lon.Inf.Bde. is allotted all billeting accommodation available in the area MARAIS - LE CROIX DE FER - LA MOTTE - RUE DE BETHUNE.

The allotment to the 6th Lon.Inf.Bde. will be issued later.

(f). CONTROL POSTS.

Control posts and Guards west of the allotted front and north of the Canal, now maintained by the 2nd Division, will be taken over by 3 p.m. 24th April as follows :-
```
        ECLUSE D'ESSARS   -   X.19.a.
        HALTE.        .   -   W.24.c.
        HALTE.        .   -   W.30.c.
```
Instructions have already been issued to all concerned with reference to these.

Medical.	3.	The 4th London Field Ambulance will remain at RAIMBERT, and the 5th London Field Ambulance at ALLOUAGNE, until further orders.

        The 6th London Field Ambulance will march on 26th April, at 8 a.m., to BETHUNE, and will billet and open at ECOLE MICHELET.

        The Bearer Division of this unit will take over the existing Advanced Dressing Station at TUNING FORK (F.5.a) from 2nd Division, and will open a new Advanced Dressing Station at LE TOURET (X.16.d) by 10 a.m. 25th April, and will evacuate to the 5th Field Ambulance until the 6th London Field Ambulance has opened.

        This unit will be responsible for clearing the area occupied by the 5th and 6th London Infantry Brigades.

        The Divisional Sanitary Section will march to BETHUNE on 24th April at 1 p.m.

        The Motor Ambulance Workshop unit will remain at LAPUGNOY until arrangements are completed for its move to BETHUNE.

Supply.	4.	Supply Refilling Point will be at BETHUNE.
Reports.	5.	Divisional Report Centre will close at MENSECQ at 2 p.m. 24th April, and will re-open at building now occupied by the 2nd Division Signals (Marche aux Poulets, BETHUNE) at the same hour.

                                                Wm Thwaites
                                                      Lt.Colonel,
                                                   General Staff,
                                                 London Division.

Issued at 10 p.m. :-

    Copy No. 1. Operation Order File.
      ,,   2.   ,,
      ,,   3.   ,,
      ,,   4.   ,,
      ,,   5. A.A.&Q.M.G.
      ,,   6. 5th Lon.Inf.Brigade.
      ,,   7. 6th Lon.Inf.Brigade.
      ,,   8. G.O.C.,R.A.
      ,,   9. C.R.E.
      ,,   10. London Cyclist Company.
      ,,   11. London Signal Company.
      ,,   12. A.D.M.S.
      ,,   13. O.C. London Train.
      ,,   14. A.P.M.
      ,,   15. Town Commandant, BETHUNE.
      ,,   16. 1st Corps.
      ,,   17. 1st Division.
      ,,   18. 2nd Division.
      ,,   19. 4th Lon.Inf.Bde.

4th Lon. Inf. Bde. G.S.C. W^d Bat. C^d 4th London Bde 25/4/15.

5th Lon. Inf. Bde.
___

In forwarding attached reports on the battalions under your command I am instructed by the G.O.C. to say that the question of the responsibility of Officers and N.C.O's is to be impressed upon them and that the strictest supervision is to be maintained over sanitation.

I append the following general report by the G.O.C. 2nd Division for your information and guidance :-

> " The rank and file promise well and now only require experience. The officers have not in all cases realized the importance of their duties whilst in the front line, especially as regards responsibility for vigilance on the part of the men, for maintenance and repair of trenches and parapets, and <u>for sanitation.</u> "

Kindly return the reports.

                         Lt.Colonel,
23rd April 1915.   General Staff,
                         Lon. Div.

E.D.No.2/9/G.

2. *Confidential*

Headquarters 5th London Inf. Brigade.

Complied with, and passed.

             P. Cuthbert
             Brig: General
       Com^{dg} 4th London Inf. Brigade

3

Headquarters London Division.

Noted and returned

            George Nugent Brig Gen.
            Com^g 5th London J. Bde

BM 388
27.4.15.

> 2nd DIVISION
> GENERAL STAFF
> No. G.S. 304/7.
> Date............

1st Corps.

I forward the reports of the G.O.C. 4th, 5th, and 6th Brigades on the battalions of the 2nd London Division which have been attached for training.

The rank and file promise well and now only require experience. The officers have not in all cases realized the importance of their duties whilst in the front line, especially as regards responsibility for vigilance on the part of the men, for maintenance and repair of trenches and parapets, and for sanitation.

(Sgd) H S Horne.

22nd April 1915.

Major-General.

Commanding 2nd Division.

FILE COPY.

4th Lon. Inf. Bde.
5th Lon. Inf. Bde.

In forwarding attached reports on the battalions under your command I am instructed by the G.O.C. to say that the question of the responsibility of Officers and N.C.O's is to be impressed upon them and that the strictest supervision is to be maintained over sanitation.

I append the following general report by the G.O.C. 2nd Division for your information and guidance :-

> " The rank and file promise well and now only require experience. The officers have not in all cases realized the importance of their duties whilst in the front line, especially as regards responsibility for vigilance on the part of the men, for maintenance and repair of trenches and parapets, and for sanitation. "

Kindly return the reports.

Lt.Colonel,
General Staff,
Lon. Div.

23rd April 1915.

L.D.No.2/9/G.

1st Corps No. 251 (G).

London Division.

The enclosed reports on the 15th, 17th, 18th, 19th and 20th Battalions, London Regiment, are forwarded for your information.

R.W.Whigham   Brig. General.

22nd April, 1915.   General Staff, 1st Corps.

"A" Form.
Army Form C. 2121.
MESSAGES AND SIGNALS.

TO: London Div
26/15

Sender's Number: GA 41
Day of Month: 24th
AAA

Advantage must be taken of periods during which troops of 5th and 6th brigades and 4th London brigade are in reserve to rehearse in detail the actual assault from entrenchments particularly getting into and out of forming up places aaa This is being done with excellent results by 1st Div near LE VERT BOIS farm Q 35 d aaa to avoid damage to crops in other places it is suggested that 2nd Div and 4th London brigade should use 1st Div breastworks at that place by mutual arrangement as regards repair of damage done to parapets addressed 2nd and London Divs repeated 1st Div

From
Place: 1st Corps
Time: 1 pm

R Whigham BGGS

Wt. W1154/2240. 7/11. 7,500,000. Sch. 4a.   "A" Form.   Army Form C. 2121.
MESSAGES AND SIGNALS.   No. of Message _____

Prefix	Code	m.	Words	Charge	This message is on a/c of:	Recd. at	m.
Office of Origin and Service Instructions.			Sent			Date	
			At	m.	Service.	From	
			To				
			By		(Signature of "Franking Officer.")	By	

TO Secret   4th Lon Inf Brig

Sender's Number.	Day of Month	In reply to Number	
* 76/15	24th		A A A

1st Corps instruct us that advantage must be taken of period during which 4th Lon Inf Brig is in reserve to rehearse in detail the actual assault from entrenchments particularly getting into and out of forming up places aaa 1st Corps suggests that arrangements might be made for the use of 1st Divn trenches near LE VERBOIS farm Q.3.5.d where they are practising aaa It is however pointed out that there are trenches constructed near LAPUGNOY which you can use.

From Lon Div
Place BETHUNE
Time 5.12 m

"A" Form.   Army Form C. 2121.
MESSAGES AND SIGNALS.

Prefix......Code......m.	Words	Charge	This message is on a/c of:	Recd. at......m.
Office of Origin and Service Instructions	Sent At......m.		Service.	Date 26/11 From......
	To...... By......		(Signature of "Franking Officer.")	By......

TO

Sender's Number.	Day of Month.	In reply to Number.	
GA 42	24th		AAA

Following arrangements as regards
1st Army and 1st Corps Reserves
will come into effect at once aaa
1st Army Reserve - 1st Guards Bde
aaa 1st Corps Reserve - the
infantry brigade of 2nd Div billeted in
BETHUNE and 4th London Bde
area acknowledge aaa addsd
1st 2nd and London Divs

Lon Div/270
8.45 pm

From 1st Corps
Place
Time 8 pm

"A" Form.　　Army Form C. 2121.

MESSAGES AND SIGNALS.

Prefix	Code	m.	Words	Charge	This message is on a/c of:	Recd. at ____ m.

Office of Origin and Service Instructions

Sent At ____ m.　　Service.　　Date ____

Scout　　To ____　　From ____

By ____　　(Signature of "Franking Officer.")　　By ____

TO　　4th Lon Inf Brig

Sender's Number.	Day of Month.	In reply to Number	
G 75/17	24th		AAA

Your brigade has been placed in Corps Reserve aaa acknowledge

From　　4 Lon Div
Place　　BETHUNE
Time　　9.40 pm

(Z)

Censor.　　Signature of Addresser or person authorised to telegraph in his name.

* This line should be erased if not required.

SPECIAL INSTRUCTIONS TO ARTILLERY.

With regard to the arrangements now being made in connection with the proposed operations by 1st Army, the artillery arrangements should be such that our guns are disposed with the following objects in view :-

1. Firstly -
   (a). To enable the 1st and Indian Corps to break through the German line about RICHEBOURG L'AVOUE and advance to and secure the line RUE DU MARAIS - LORGIES - LIGNY-le-PETIT.
   (b). To enable the 4th Corps to break through the German line about ROUGES BANCS and advance to and secure FROMELLES and the FROMELLES - AUBERS road.
   (c). To bring sufficient artillery fire to bear to hold the enemy on that portion of the line which is not being attacked, particularly between NEUVE CHAPELLE and FAUQUISSART, both inclusive.

2. Secondly -
   To cover the advance of the Indian Corps on LIGNY-le-GRAND and the 4th Corps on LA CLIQUETERIE FARM, with a view to securing that high ground.

3. Thirdly -
   Covering the subsequent advance of our troops through ILLIES on DON.

   It will also be necessary to arrange for sufficient counter-batteries to silence the enemy's artillery during

all

all the above stages.

With regard to paras: 2 and 3, it is probable that the German defences on the ridge about AUBERS - LA CLIQUETERIE FM. - HAUT POMMEREAU and LIGNY-le-GRAND may be strongly held, and that they will have guns further to the east in support of the infantry holding these defences.

The capture of this ridge is essential for the success of our subsequent advance on DON, and special attention should be given to providing strong artillery support to our attack on this ridge.

(sd) R. BUTLER, Brigadier-General
24th April, 1915.   General Staff, 1st Army.

G/2/10

1ST ARMY CORPS
GENERAL STAFF
(OPERATIONS SECTION)
No. 251 (G)
Date

CONFIDENTIAL.

London Division.

The attached copies of reports of commanding officers of battalions to which companies of the 23rd Battalion London Regiment were attached, from 11th to 15th April, 1915, are forwarded for information.

24th April, 1915.   Rholyhaven   Brig-General,
General Staff, 1st Corps.

2

G.O.C.,
    6th Lon.Inf.Brigade.
====================================

Forwarded for your information and return.

I am requested by the G.O.C. to say that the O.C. 23rd Battalion should be instructed to give very special attention to the points referred to in the reports of Lt.Colonel Stewart and Major Craig Brown.

Lt.Colonel
GENERAL STAFF
LONDON DIVISION

CONFIDENTIAL.   1st Divn: No: 201 (G).

Headquarters,
         1st Division.

         I beg to forward herewith Commanding Officers'
reports on companies of the 23rd Battalion The London Regt:
attached to my Brigade from the 11th to 15th April, 1915.

H.Q., 1st Guards Bde: (Sd) H.C.Lowther, Brig-Genl.
22nd April, 1915.   Commanding 1st Guards Brigade.

                              2.

Headquarters,
         1st Corps.

         I forward the attached reports which give a clear
idea of the state of efficiency of this battalion. I would
particularly call attention to the remarks at "A" in Lt-Colonel
Stewart's report, and at "B" in Major Craig-Brown's report, ~~also "C" in Lt-Colonel Green's report~~. These are the points
where improvement is required.

24th April, 1915.   (Sd) R.Haking, Major-General,
                                   Commanding 1st Division.

SECRET.

1st CORPS INSTRUCTIONS (2).
----

289 (G). 25th April, 1915.

1. In continuation of 1st Corps Secret Instructions 289 (G), dated 20th April, the following is an outline of the intentions of the Lieut. General Commanding as regards the action of the 1st Corps as a whole.

2. The task of the troops under G.O.C. London Division is to maintain their right at GIVENCHY and CUINCHY, and to be prepared to take advantage of any weakening of the enemy in their front to occupy RUE D'OUVERT, and to relieve the troops of the 1st Division at "THE ORCHARD" (S.21.c.), LA QUINQUE RUE, and RUE DU MARAIS, when those points have been secured.

3. The troops under G.O.C. 2nd Division will be held in readiness to :-
   (i) Support the 1st Division, particularly in gaining its second objective, RUE DU MARAIS and the LA BASSEE - ESTAIRES road.
  (ii) To fill a gap between 1st Division and Indian Corps as the advance progresses.
 (iii) To confirm the success of 1st Division and push on through ILLIES and LA MOTTELETTE.

4. During the night immediately preceding the attack, mines will be exploded under the German trenches opposite GIVENCHY and CUINCHY, unless the action of the enemy has made it necessary to explode them earlier.

5. On the morning selected for the attack, and, if the light permits, before the hour fixed for the general bombardment to begin, the 15 pr. and 18 pr. batteries of the London Division will open fire on previously selected points in the hostile wire entanglements in front of CUINCHY, LE PLANTIN, and FESTUBERT, with the double object of drawing the fire of the enemy's guns away from the wire cutting batteries of 1st Division, and of cutting gaps in his wire opposite FESTUBERT which may be useful in the event of an advance by the London Infantry Brigades.
    The subsequent action of the artillery at disposal of G.O.C. London Division will be co-ordinated with that of the artillery supporting the attack, particularly with a view to dealing with the development of hostile counter-attacks from RUE D'OUVERT and VIOLAINES. The 26th Heavy Battery, R.G.A., will be responsible for engaging hostile batteries from VIOLAINES (inclusive) to the south.
    A table showing the objectives of the artillery supporting 1st Division, and the sequence in which they are to be engaged, will be issued later.

6. As regards the attack of the 1st Division, it is imperative that the left brigade should keep touch with the troops of the Indian Corps attacking LA TOURELLE and the DISTILLERY, and be prepared to assist them in capturing that locality.

7. The following are the arrangements as regards the co-operation of the Royal Flying Corps :-

   (i) For observation of artillery fire there will be two wireless machines allotted to 1st Division. Two other machines with signalling lamps will be allotted to London Division for work in connection with 26th Heavy Battery, R.G.A.

(ii).

(ii) For tactical reconnaissance :-

    (a) Two machines (not fitted with wireless) will be at the disposal of 1st Corps. There will be a message dropping station close to Advanced 1st Corps Report Centre, which will also be in telephonic communication with R.F.C. landing ground.

    (b) Four wireless machines will be controlled from 1st Army Headquarters with several ground stations at which messages will be received direct from the air. One of these stations will be close to 1st Division Report Centre (X.4.b.), whence the information will be transmitted to Advanced 1st Division and Advanced 1st Corps.

    (c) Requests for tactical information to be obtained by air reconnaissance must be addressed through the Signal Service to "Advanced 1st Corps" and not to the ground wireless station which is a receiving station only.

R. Whigham Brig. General.
General Staff, 1st Corps.

"A" Form. Army Form C. 2121.

MESSAGES AND SIGNALS.

TO
5th Lon Inf Brig
6th Lon Inf Brig

Sender's Number: GB 294
Day of Month: Twenty-fifth
AAA

Following battalions are placed in Divisional Reserve aaa They are available for working parties and will take their turn in your scheme of reliefs aaa Batⁿ of 5th Lon Inf Brig quartered at GORRE – LA CROIX DE FER and Batⁿ of 6th Lon Inf Brig quartered at ESSARS – LES FACONS aaa The designation of the units so quartered will be reported when relief takes place aaa aeth⁰ Judge aaa addressed 5th and 6th Lon Inf Brigs

From: Lon Div
Place:
Time: 10·20 am

Wt. W1154/2240. 7/11. 7,500,000. Sch. 4a.　　"A" Form.　　　　　Army Form C. 2121.

MESSAGES AND SIGNALS.

No. of Message _____

Prefix ___ Code ___ m.	Words	Charge	This message is on a/c of:	Recd. at ___ m.
Office of Origin and Service Instructions.	Sent At ___ m. To By		___ Service. (Signature of "Franking Officer.")	Date ___ From ___ By

TO	First Corps
	First Div
	Second Div

Sender's Number.	Day of Month	In reply to Number	
* GB 304	Twenty five		A A A

Situation report All quiet nothing to
report AAA Addressed First Corps repeated
First and Second Divs.

From Lon. Div.
Place
Time 5.37 pm.

The above may be forwarded as now corrected.　(Z)

Censor.　Signature of Addressor or person authorised to telegraph in his name.

* This line should be erased if not required.

"A" Form.   Army Form C. 2121.

MESSAGES AND SIGNALS.   No. of Message_____

Prefix___ Code ___ m.	Words	Charge	This message is on a/c of:	Recd. at_____ m.
Office of Origin and Service Instructions.	Sent		_____Service.	Date_____
	At_____ m.			From_____
	To_____			
	By_____		(Signature of "Franking Officer.")	By_____

TO: First Div.

Sender's Number.	Day of Month.	In reply to Number	AAA
G.H 290	25th		

Ref Q 264 Can you arrange for a proportion of R.A personnel now working four inch trench mortars to remain with the two mortars handed over to this division for a few days until our personnel are acquainted with the weapons.

From: Lou Div
Place:
Time: 9.15 a.m.

The above may be forwarded as now corrected. (Z)

Censor.   Signature of Addressee or person authorised to telegraph in his name.

* This line should be erased if not required.

"C" Form (Duplicate). Army Form C. 2123.
MESSAGES AND SIGNALS.

No. of Message

Charges to Pay £ s. d.

Office Stamp: 25.IV.15

Service Instructions.

Handed in at 1st Div. Office 2.24 m. Received 2.43 p.m.

TO London Divn

Sender's Number	Day of Month	In reply to Number	
Q277	25th	QH290	AAA

RA personnel will remain with mortars

L.D. 303
11.30 p.m.
From Q.
M.H. 3.14

FROM PLACE & TIME 1st Div 2.20 p.m.

Army Form C. 398.

London Division
Appendices to War Diary (GS)
April 25th — 26th

To:—

DESPATCH.	RECEIPT.
Sender's No.	Date .... hour .... m.
Date .... hour .... m.	Signature:—

URGENT or ORDINARY.

"A" Form. Army Form C. 2121.

MESSAGES AND SIGNALS.

TO	First Corps	

Sender's Number.	Day of Month.	In reply to Number	AAA
G.B. 291	Twenty five	G.A. 43	

Reliefs are fully completed

From: LoN Div.
Place:
Time: 9-33 am

H.R. Hunt Capt G.S.

G/111

45

From O.C. Signal Coy
London Div'n

To Head Qrs
London Div'n

Copy No. 17 of Secret
Letter G/111 received

26/4/15
26/4/15

L Alexander MAJOR,
O. C. SIGNAL Co.
LONDON DIVISION.

TACTICAL PROGRESS REPORT OF LONDON DIVISION

up to Noon 25th April, 1915.
****

OPERATIONS.   1.   Trenches in rear of Section D.1, shelled at 4 p.m. yesterday.

RUE DE BOIS shelled between 12 noon and 2 p.m. yesterday.

WORK.   2.   Front line of C.1 and C.2 improved and strengthened

Communication Trench commenced West of INDIAN VILLAGE, parapet and parades where existing improved.

D.1.c and d - parapet improved.

No.G/51/5

25th April 1915.

(sd) B.Burnett-Hitchcock,
Major,
for Major General,
Commanding London Division T.F.

SECRET.

Copy No. 2

Amendments to :-

Lon.Div. Secret Memo No.G/111, dated 26th April, 1915.

❋❋❋❋❋❋❋❋❋❋❋

Page 2, paragraph 5 (ii), line 8. Dele from "The place of

deployment ...." to end of (ii), and substitute:-

"These reserves will be assembled in close proximity to
the supporting line, viz - LE PLANTIN - FESTUBERT -
RUE DE L'EPINETTE. From these positions, the exact
site of which will be selected by Infantry Brigade
Commanders, the Brigade Reserves are available to
complete the action of local counterstrokes or, in
case of extreme necessity should the enemy break
through the line in strength, to occupy this supporting
line which they would hold at all costs."

Paragraph 5 (iii). Dele whole para and substitute :-

"Divisional Reserves are maintained under the orders of
the Divisional Commander for the purpose of a general
counter attack in force in whichever section he may
select. They are billeted some way back in order to
ensure complete rest, but have rendezvous appointed
to which they would move on receipt of orders. These
rendezvous are known to Infantry Brigade Commanders.
The G.O.C. has authorised Inf.Bde.Commanders to use
the battalions of the Divisional Reserve without
further reference in case of extreme necessity.
They would report their action. "

❋❋❋❋❋❋❋❋❋❋❋❋❋❋❋❋❋

The above amendments to Lon.Div.Secret Memo

No.G/111, dated 26th April 1915, are forwarded for your

information. Kindly acknowledge receipt.

H.R. Hunt

No.G/111/2

29th April 1915.

Captain,
General Staff
for Major General
Commanding London Divn.

SECRET.

Headquarters
   1st Corps.
==================

           The attached copy of Secret Memorandum No. Lon.Div.
G/111, is forwarded for information.

                                          Lt.Colonel,
                                      for Major General,
                                  Commanding London Division.

SECRET.   Copy No. 2

LONDON DIVISION.

Principles for Defence of FESTUBERT and RUE De L'EPINETTE
("C" and "D.1") Sections, and eventually to include
GIVENCHY and CUINCHY ("B" and "A") Sections.

General principles.	1.(a).	The front line of trenches or breastworks to be held at all costs.
	(b).	Should any portion of the front line be broken, the remainder of the line will hold on.
	(c).	Local counter attack will be delivered at once to regain any of the line temporarily lost. Should this prove insufficient it will hold on to whatever line it makes good until counter attack by Brigade or, if necessary, Divisional Reserve can be delivered.

The infantry are therefore disposed in two main divisions :-

(i). For defensive action :-

    (a). Troops in front line trenches or breastworks, including those in their immediate support.
    (b). Garrisons of Supporting Points.

(ii). For offensive action :-

    Local battalion reserves.
    Brigade reserves.
    Divisional reserves.

Front line.	2.	The front line must be capable of being fully manned without any delay, and cover must be provided for as many of the garrison as possible during a bombardment.
Supporting Points.	3.	Supporting Points, constructed for all round defence, close in rear of the front line are to be permanently garrisoned. Their action, should the front line be broken, is to hold out to the last man in order to delay the further advance of the enemy, to fire on his attempts to establish himself on the ground he has gained, to break up his attack if he attempts to penetrate between the Supporting Points, and to assist the counter attack. Garrisons of Supporting Points will NOT counter attack.
Counter attacks.	4.	All officers will base their action on the established fact that the most effective counterstroke is that made by companies, always held in readiness to support the front line immediately the front line is broken.

Positions of reserves.

5.(i). Local reserves must be so placed that their offensive action can be set in motion without any delay. Rehearsals by day and night must therefore be held and the part which each is to play must be known to all ranks.

Cover from fire under which these reserves can be deployed must be so constructed as not to impede rapid offensive action across the open. Communication trenches must also be provided up which they can be moved with the utmost rapidity, under cover, if time permits.

To assist their offensive, the ground in rear of the first line must be under the fire of Supporting Points in which machine guns are placed for the purpose, whenever available.

To add to the effectiveness of this supporting fire, entanglements should be prepared in rear of front line so as to break up the enemy's attack, if the hostile troops have been successful in crossing the front line, and to cause them to advance in directions which bring them under the fire of the Supporting Points.

(ii). Brigade Reserves are necessarily placed in accordance with accommodation available. They should be capable of turning out at short notice and will move to their place of deployment without further orders. It is therefore essential that the routes to be followed to the position of deployment are known and also well marked. These should be screened from view. The place of deployment will be the second line of defence which they will occupy and hold at all costs should the local counter attacks have failed to arrest the enemy's advance. They are there available to complete the action of local counterstrokes or to deliver a general counterstroke.

(iii). Divisional Reserves are further back for the purposes of resting. Their lines of approach to every section of the defence are to be reconnoitred and well marked.

Communications.

6. The essential factor for the maintenance of the front line is good communication, to ensure timely notice to the supports and reserves, to superior authority and to the supporting artillery, of any attack. It is the duty, therefore, of commanders to establish alternative methods of communication, and of all ranks to protect wires from damage. All officers must be made acquainted with the systems and, where necessary, telephone lines are to be <u>buried under the supervision of the signal service.</u>

Points of attack.

7. The most important portion of our front against which an attack is most likely to be delivered is :-

(i). In the vicinity of the ORCHARD (S.21.c.) in Section D.1 where the enemy's trenches closely approach our own, where the enemy's assaulting troops would have a very short distance to go, and where there is a salient in our line.

At

At this and other weak places, increased depth of entanglement should be constructed and where possible some at least of it should be concealed from the enemy's view.

Execution of works and R.E.

8. Every endeavour must be made to relieve the Royal Engineers of all work that can be done by infantry working parties.

All wiring, trench and breastwork can perfectly well be carried out by infantry, and it should be a point of honour with all ranks that they are independent of outside assistance for the execution of these works to which they are trained.

Brigade workshops should be formed under the direction of the R.E. for the preparation of trench stores, including periscopes, masks, etc.

The Royal Engineers should only be called in for special tasks requiring technical knowledge or very rapid execution, and infantry brigade commanders, in consultation with the C.R.E., will see that the work required is explained at once, so as to allow of the preparation of the necessary materials without delay.

Royal Artillery.

9. Close co-operation with the infantry, the support of whom is their primary function, is essential for all battery officers. Their observing stations should be made known to relieving infantry and their requirements for observation under varying circumstances should be explained. These requirements will be completed in co-operation with infantry commanders.

The C.R.A. is responsible for complete and accurate registration and that the necessary data is always instantly available for fire to be opened when support is called for. He is also responsible for giving additional artillery support to any threatened point should it be required, and for the necessary registration having been completed, and further arranging mutual support with neighbouring divisions.

Offensive action.

10. It is to be remembered that the surest defence is to maintain a continuous superiority over the enemy and this is attained by better snipers, more active patrols, keener listening patrols, and by constant reconnaissance of his front line and of any movement in rear of it.

Firing line.

11. Although loopholes may be used for snipers and although head cover is necessary for machine guns and their detachments, in case of attack every man will fire over the parapet. For this purpose constant supervision over the firing platform is necessary so that repairs may be made at once, and that the maximum number of men may be accommodated in the firing line.

Every man should be familiar with the exact spot which he is to occupy at the parapet.

Schemes of defence.

12. Sub-section commanders will study their areas and frame plans for action from the point of view of :-

(a). Any portion of their line being broken.

(b). The neighbouring sub-section being broken.

Their plans will show :-

(i). Normal distribution of the infantry.

(ii). Action by the infantry in case of attack.

(iii). Communication trenches or additional works or wiring required.

(iv). Rapid communications with brigade headquarters, neighbouring sub-sections, and supporting batteries.

(v). Action by machine guns, including the preparation of alternative positions for them.

(vi). Supply and storage of hand grenades, S.A.A., Supplies, and water. Care is to be taken that the stock of water should be constantly "turned over".

These plans will be co-ordinated by infantry brigade commanders who will consult with the officers commanding the supporting artillery. Works to be carried out should be put in hand at once.

Similarly, infantry brigade commanders will prepare plans and submit them to Divisional Headquarters, including in them the details of artillery support.

It is essential that all officers be intimately acquainted with the plans of the area in which they operate, and that all ranks should know beforehand what they are to do when they first take up their duties, whether as trench or supporting point garrison, or as part of the mobile supports, or reserves.

Great attention is to be paid to the proper maintenance and care of masks and of the solution of bi-carbonate of potash intended to neutralize the effect of poisonous gases.

[signature]

Major,
for Lt.Colonel,
General Staff,
London Division.

No.G/112.

26th April, 1915.

"A" Form.
MESSAGES AND SIGNALS.

Army Form C. 2121.

TO: LON DIV — 1.35 pm

Sender's Number: BM/634 Day of Month: 26th AAA

the 1st DIV have allotted the 5th LON FAB a definite task which they are now in process of registering AAA as soon as they have completed this it is necessary for them to register the zones which cover the front of the 6th LON INF BDE AAA support of course be night cannot if the 6th LON given to the INF BDE until the zone in their front has been completely registered AAA I therefore request as a special case that 6 rounds per gun

"A" Form.
MESSAGES AND SIGNALS.
Army Form C. 2121.

be	allotted	in	lieu	of
3	per	gun	for	the
week	ending	Saturday	May	1st
AAA				

From: LON DIV ARTY
Time: 1.15 pm

L Div/346
1.35 pm

"A" Form.
Army Form C. 2121.

MESSAGES AND SIGNALS.

No. of Message _____

Prefix _____ Code _____ m.	Words	Charge	This message is on a/c of:	Recd. at _____ m.
Office of Origin and Service Instructions	Sent			Date _____
	At _____ m.		_____ Service.	From _____
	To _____			
	By _____		(Signature of "Franking Officer.")	By _____

| TO | 1st Corps | | |

| Sender's Number. | Day of Month. | In reply to Number | AAA |
| * GB 319 | Twenty six | | |

Following from CRA Lon. Div. begins AAA
The 1st Div have allotted the 5th Lon. F.A.B. a definite
task which they are now in process of registering AAA
As soon as they have completed this it is
necessary for them to register the zones which
cover the front of the 6th Lon Inf. Bde AAA
Support at night cannot of course be given
to the 6th Lon Inf Bde until the zone in
their front has been completely registered AAA
I therefore request as a special case that
6 rounds per gun be allotted in lieu of
3 per gun for the week ending Saturday
May 1st AAA ends AAA Strongly recommend
this application

From Lon. Div.
Place
Time 2.25 p.m.

"C" Form (Duplicate).   Army Form C. 2123.
MESSAGES AND SIGNALS.

Handed in at ACO   Office 7.0   Received 8.3

TO London Div

Sender's Number	Day of Month	In reply to Number	
Q295	26th	95319	AAA

Any rounds absolutely necessary but not exceeding six rounds per gun for registration may be expended daily by 5th London FA Bde Coh further instructions will follow

LD/330
7.6 pm

FROM 1st Corps
PLACE & TIME 6.50 pm

"A" Form.
Army Form C. 2121.

MESSAGES AND SIGNALS.

No. of Message_____

Prefix____ Code____ m.	Words	Charge	This message is on a/c of:	Recd. at_____ m.
Office of Origin and Service Instructions.				Date_____
	Sent		Service.	From_____
	At_____ m.			
	To_____			
	By_____		(Signature of "Franking Officer.")	By_____

TO LON. DIV ARTY

| Sender's Number. | Day of Month. | In reply to Number | AAA |
| GB 324 | Twenty six | PM/637 | |

1st Corps wire begins AAA Any rounds absolutely necessary but not exceeding six rounds per gun for registration may be expended daily by 5th Lon. FA Bde AAA Further instructions will follow. AAA ends.

From LON. DIV
Place
Time 7.15 pm.

The above may be forwarded as now corrected.   (Z)

Censor.   Signature of Addresser or person authorised to telegraph in his name.

* This line should be erased if not required.

"A" Form.
MESSAGES AND SIGNALS.

Army Form C. 2121.

No. of Message _____

Prefix _____ Code _____ m.	Words	Charge	This message is on a/c of:	Recd. at _____ m.
Office of Origin and Service Instructions.				Date _____
	Sent		_____ Service.	From _____
	At _____ m.			
	To _____			
	By _____		(Signature of "Franking Officer.")	By _____

TO { Fifth | Lon | Inf | Bde

| Sender's Number. | Day of Month. | In reply to Number | AAA |
| G.H 323 | 26th | | |

left of Guards Brigade marked by traverse in Breastwork between C1 and B Sections AAA There is only one traverse on this Breastwork AAA G.O.C. 4th Guards Brigade instructed to mark this point with a signboard

From Lon Div
Place
Time 7 p.m.

The above may be forwarded as now corrected. (Z)

Censor. H.R. Hunt Capt G.S.
Signature of Addressor or person authorised to telegraph in his name.

* This line should be erased if not required.

"A" Form.
MESSAGES AND SIGNALS.
Army Form C. 2121.

TO: LONDON DIV

Sender's Number	Day of Month	In reply to Number	AAA
BM648	26		

Have spoken to Colonel Mony direct AAA He has registered a portion of SIXTH Inf Bde front this afternoon AAA

LD 336
8.30 pm

From: LONDON DIV ARTY
Time: 8/0

(Z) Cyril Wray
Bri Genl.

"A" Form.
Army Form C. 2121.

MESSAGES AND SIGNALS.

No. of Message_____

Prefix	Code	m	Words	Charge	This message is on a/c of:	Recd. at_____m.
Office of Origin and Service Instructions			Sent			Date
			At _____ m		_____ Service	From
			To			By
			By		(Signature of "Franking Officer.")	

TO	Fifth	don	Inf	Bde
	Sixth	don	Inf	Bde
	don	Div.	Cyclists.	

| Sender's Number. | Day of Month. | In reply to Number | AAA |
| G. H 328 | 26th | | |

Each Platoon of Div. Cyclist Company will carry out a tour of 48 hours in the trenches for instructional purposes AAA Three Platoons will be attached in turn to each Infantry Brigade now in front line AAA Arrangements for attachment will be made direct between Infantry Brigades & Cyclist Company AAA Dates of attachment will be notified to this office AAA Each Platoon during it's tour will become acquainted with the whole of the Brigade front AAA Addressed Fifth & sixth don. Inf. Bdes don Cyclist Coy.

From	don	Div		
Place				
Time	10 p.m			

The above may be forwarded as now corrected. (Z) H R Hunt Capt G.S.

Censor.   Signature of Addressor or person authorised to telegraph in his name.

* This line should be erased if not required.

TACTICAL PROGRESS REPORT OF LONDON DIVISION
up to Noon 26th April, 1915.

OPERATIONS. 1. RUE DU BOIS shelled between 12 noon and 2 p.m. 25th.

15th Lon. Battery fired during night 25th/26th on parties working on work K.

71st Battery R.F.A. fired on SNIPERS HOUSE during the night.

WORK. 2. Work of filling in breastwork connecting Section C(1) with Section B continued.

Breastwork in C(2) continued.

Work carried out on Communication trenches in D1 c and d.

Front line trenches in Section D improved.

INFORMATION. 3. Germans working in square S 20 d. Earth seen to be thrown up.

Enemy in front of C2 shouted across to our men that neither we nor they wanted to fight and that we should wait till May 15th.

German troops opposite D1 c and d appear to have been relieved during night of 25th/26th. Considerable shouting was heard in these trenches before work was commenced.

Patrols report that enemy were strengthening their wire opposite Section D.

L.D. G/51/5

Major General,
Commanding London Division, T.F.

SECRET.　　　　　　　　　　　　　　　　　　　Copy No. 20

LONDON DIVISION.

Principles for Defence of FESTUBERT and RUE De L'EPINETTE ("C" and "D.1") Sections, and eventually to include GIVENCHY and CUINCHY ("B" and "A") Sections.

General principles.
1. (a).　The front line of trenches or breastworks to be held at all costs.

 (b).　Should any portion of the front line be broken, the remainder of the line will hold on.

 (c).　Local counter attack will be delivered at once to regain any of the line temporarily lost. Should this prove insufficient it will hold on to whatever line it makes good until counter attack by Brigade or, if necessary, Divisional Reserve can be delivered.

The infantry are therefore disposed in two main Divisions :-

(i). For defensive action :-

 (a). Troops in front line trenches or breastworks, including those in their immediate support.
 (b). Garrisons of Supporting Points.

(ii). For offensive action :-

 Local battalion reserves.
 Brigade reserves.
 Divisional reserves.

Front line.
2.　The front line must be capable of being fully manned without any delay, and cover must be provided for as many of the garrison as possible during a bombardment.

Supporting Points.
3.　Supporting Points, constructed for all round defence, close in rear of the front line are to be permanently garrisoned. Their action, should the front line be broken, is to hold out to the last man in order to delay the further advance of the enemy, to fire on his attempts to establish himself on the ground he has gained, to break up his attack if he attempts to penetrate between the Supporting Points, and to assist the counter attack.
 Garrisons of Supporting Points will NOT counter attack.

Counter attacks.
4.　All officers will base their action on the established fact that the most effective counterstroke is that made by companies, always held in readiness to support the front line immediately the front line is broken.

Positions of reserves.

5.(i). Local reserves must be so placed that their offensive action can be set in motion without any delay. Rehearsals by day and night must therefore be held and the part which each is to play must be known to all ranks.

Cover from fire under which these reserves can be deployed must be so constructed as not to impede rapid offensive action across the open. Communication trenches must also be provided up which they can be moved with the utmost rapidity, under cover, if time permits.

To assist their offensive, the ground in rear of the first line must be under the fire of Supporting Points in which machine guns are placed for the purpose, whenever available.

To add to the effectiveness of this supporting fire, entanglements should be prepared in rear of front line so as to break up the enemy's attack, if the hostile troops have been successful in crossing the front line, and to cause them to advance in directions which bring them under the fire of the Supporting Points.

(ii). Brigade Reserves are necessarily placed in accordance with accommodation available. They should be capable of turning out at short notice and will move to their place of deployment without further orders. It is therefore essential that the routes to be followed to the position of deployment are known and also well marked. These should be screened from view. The place of deployment will be the second line of defence which they will occupy and hold at all costs should the local counter attacks have failed to arrest the enemy's advance. They are there available to complete the action of local counterstrokes or to deliver a general counterstroke.

(iii). Divisional Reserves are further back for the purposes of resting. Their lines of approach to every section of the defence are to be reconnoitred and well marked.

Communications.

6. The essential factor for the maintenance of the front line is good communication, to ensure timely notice to the supports and reserves, to superior authority and to the supporting artillery, of any attack. It is the duty, therefore, of commanders to establish alternative methods of communication, and of all ranks to protect wires from damage. All officers must be made acquainted with the systems and, where necessary, telephone lines are to be <u>buried under the supervision of the signal service.</u>

Points of attack.

7. The most important portion of our front against which an attack is most likely to be delivered is :-

(i). In the vicinity of the ORCHARD (S.21.c.) in Section D.1 where the enemy's trenches closely approach our own, where the enemy's assaulting troops would have a very short distance to go, and where there is a salient in our line.

At

At this and other weak places, increased depth of entanglement should be constructed and where possible some at least of it should be concealed from the enemy's view.

Execution of works and R.E.

8. Every endeavour must be made to relieve the Royal Engineers of all work that can be done by infantry working parties.

All wiring, trench and breastwork can perfectly well be carried out by infantry, and it should be a point of honour with all ranks that they are independent of outside assistance for the execution of these works to which they are trained.

Brigade workshops should be formed under the direction of the R.E. for the preparation of trench stores, including periscopes, masks, etc.

The Royal Engineers should only be called in for special tasks requiring technical knowledge or very rapid execution, and infantry brigade commanders, in consultation with the C.R.E., will see that the work required is explained at once, so as to allow of the preparation of the necessary materials without delay.

Royal Artillery.

9. Close co-operation with the infantry, the support of whom is their primary function, is essential for all battery officers. Their observing stations should be made known to relieving infantry and their requirements for observation under varying circumstances should be explained. These requirements will be completed in co-operation with infantry commanders.

The C.R.A. is responsible for complete and accurate registration and that the necessary data is always instantly available for fire to be opened when support is called for. He is also responsible for giving additional artillery support to any threatened point should it be required, and for the necessary registration having been completed, and further arranging mutual support with neighbouring divisions.

Offensive action.

10. It is to be remembered that the surest defence is to maintain a continuous superiority over the enemy and this is attained by better snipers, more active patrols, keener listening patrols, and by constant reconnaissance of his front line and of any movement in rear of it.

Firing line.

11. Although loopholes may be used for snipers and although head cover is necessary for machine guns and their detachments, in case of attack every man will fire over the parapet. For this purpose constant supervision over the firing platform is necessary so that repairs may be made at once, and that the maximum number of men may be accommodated in the firing line.

Every man should be familiar with the exact spot which he is to occupy at the parapet.

Schemes of defence.

12. Sub-section commanders will study their areas and frame plans for action from the point of view of :-

(a). Any portion of their line being broken.

(b). The neighbouring sub-section being broken.

Their plans will show :-

(i). Normal distribution of the infantry.

(ii). Action by the infantry in case of attack.

(iii). Communication trenches or additional works or wiring required.

(iv). Rapid communications with brigade headquarters, neighbouring sub-sections, and supporting batteries.

(v). Action by machine guns, including the preparation of alternative positions for them.

(vi). Supply and storage of hand grenades, S.A.A., Supplies, and water. Care is to be taken that the stock of water should be constantly "turned over".

These plans will be co-ordinated by infantry brigade commanders who will consult with the officers commanding the supporting artillery. Works to be carried out should be put in hand at once.

Similarly, infantry brigade commanders will prepare plans and submit them to Divisional Headquarters, including in them the details of artillery support.

It is essential that all officers be intimately acquainted with the plans of the area in which they operate, and that all ranks should know beforehand what they are to do when they first take up their duties, whether as trench or supporting point garrison, or as part of the mobile supports, or reserves.

Great attention is to be paid to the proper maintenance and care of masks and of the solution of bi-carbonate of potash intended to neutralize the effect of poisonous gases.

B. Burnett Hitchcock

Major,
for Lt.Colonel,
General Staff,
London Division.

No.G/111.

26th April, 1915.

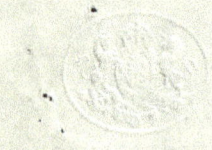

TACTICAL PROGRESS REPORT OF LONDON DIVISION

up to Noon, 27th April, 1915.

Operations. 1.   Building - bearing 104.5 from S.20 d, 0.5, and 95.5 from S.20 d, 0.3, set on fire by our guns at 11-50 a.m.   This was followed by three explosions which gave out thick black smoke.

Work.   2.   C.1. Work carried out on breastworks and drainage of front line trenches.

C.2. Front line consolidated and work done on communication trenches.

D.1. Parapets reconstructed and fire positions improved. Traverses and loopholes attended to.   Wire improved and work on communication trench continued.

Information. 3.   Searchlight seen in the direction of LA BASSEE Church at about 11 p.m. night of 26th.

Machine gun emplacement suspected opposite S.26.a 6,4 near M 2.
Two hostile guns observed by flashes on a bearing 136.5 from S.26 a 6,4; estimated range 2,200 yards.

German line opposite C 1 strongly held last night, singing continued to a late hour and working parties were heard in rear of the German line opposite C.1 at midnight.

C Barter

Major General,

Commanding London Division.

Army Form C. 398.

Appendices to War Diary
London Div'n (General Staff)
April 27th — 30th

To :—

DESPATCH.	RECEIPT.
Sender's No.	Date .... hour .... m.
Date .... hour .... m.	Signature :—

URGENT or ORDINARY.

"A" Form.   Army Form C. 2121.

MESSAGES AND SIGNALS.

| TO | ~~RE~~ LONDON DIVN. | | |

Sender's Number	Day of Month	In reply to Number	AAA
G902	27th.		

Please hand over one portable searchlight to London Divn aaa addressed RE repeats London Divn

Lon Div / 36
6-20 p.m.

From 2nd Divn
Place
Time 6.10 pm

"A" Form.
Army Form C. 2121.

MESSAGES AND SIGNALS.

No. of Message_____

Prefix____ Code____ m.	Words	Charge	This message is on a/c of:	Recd. at____ m.
Office of Origin and Service Instructions	Sent		_____Service.	Date_____
	At____ m.			From_____
	To			By_____
	By	(Signature of "Franking Officer.")		

| TO | Lon. | Div. | Engrs | |

| Sender's Number. | Day of Month. | In reply to Number | AAA |
| *USS/343 | Twenty seven | | |

Following received from Second Division begins Please hand over one portable searchlight to London Div. AAA Addressed RE repeated London Division ends AAA Please arrange to take this over

From: Lon. Div.
Place:
Time: 6.40 p.m.

The above may be forwarded as now corrected. (Z) H.R. Hunt Capt G.S.

Censor. Signature of Addressor or person authorised to telegraph in his name.

* This line should be erased if not required.

"A" Form. Army Form C. 2121.
MESSAGES AND SIGNALS.

TO: 2" London Division

Sender's Number: RE960
Day of Month: 27.4
AAA

Reference G902 from 2" Division I have instructed OC 5" Coy RE at GORRE BREWERY to hand over one searchlight.

(B 350)
LD 366
827/

From Place: CRE 2D
Time: 6.25 pm

Darling? Capt

MESSAGES AND SIGNALS.

"A" Form.   Army Form C. 2121.

Prefix ... Code ... m.	Words / Charge	This message is on a/c of:	Recd. at ... m.
Office of Origin and Service Instructions	Sent At ... m. To ... By ...	Service. (Signature of "Franking Officer.")	Date ... From ... By ...

TO: Lon. Div. Engrs.

Sender's Number.	Day of Month.	In reply to Number	AAA
G.B./350	Twenty seven		

Reference my G.H./343 today following received from C.R.E. Second Division begins Reference G/902 from 2nd Division I have instructed O/C 5th Coy. R.E. at GORRE BREWERY to hand over one searchlight AAA ends AAA

From Lon. Div.
Place
Time 9.26 pm.

The above may be forwarded as now corrected. (Z)   A.R. Hunt Capt G.S.

Signature of Addressor or person authorised to telegraph in his name.

* This line should be erased if not required.

"C" Form (Duplicate). Army Form C. 2123.
MESSAGES AND SIGNALS.

Handed in at aco

TO London Div

Sender's Number: 797
Day of Month: 27th

With reference para 2 1st Corps operation order 27 20th april the 5th London F A Bde is under the orders of GOC London Div for the present aaa Registration of targets required by 1st Div can be carried out by this Bde by Inter Divisional arrangement aaa acknowledge aaa addressed 1st Div repeated London Div

FROM: 1st Corps

"A" Form.
Army Form C. 2121.

MESSAGES AND SIGNALS.

No. of Message_____

Prefix ___ Code ___ m	Words	Charge	This message is on a/c of:	Recd. at ___ m.
Office of Origin and Service Instructions	Sent		_____Service.	Date_____
	At_____ m			From_____
	To_____		(Signature of "Franking Officer.")	By_____
	By_____			

TO { Lon | Div | Arty | }

| Sender's Number. | Day of Month. | In reply to Number | AAA |
| G.H 345 | 27th | | |

First Corps wire begins With reference para 2 1st Corps Operation Order 27 20th April the 5th London F.A. Bde is under the orders of G.O.C London Div for the present AAA Registration of targets required by 1st Div can be carried out by this Bde by Interdivisional Arrangements aaa Acknowledge aaa Addressed 1st Div repeated London Div. Wire ends AAA ⊕ Arrange for this registration to be carried out with G.O.C RA 1st Div.

From   Lon   Div
Place
Time   7.20 pm

The above may be forwarded as now corrected.   (Z)   H R Hunt Capt G.S.
Censor.   Signature of Addressor or person authorised to telegraph in his name.

* This line should be erased if not required.

"A" Form.   Army Form C. 2121.
                    MESSAGES AND SIGNALS.   No. of Message _____

TO	4th Lon M.G. Bry
	5th Lon M.G. Bry
	6th Lon M.G. Bry

Sender's Number: GB 347   Day of Month: 27th   AAA

Four machine gun detachments having been placed at the disposal of the Divn temporarily two will report to H.Qrs 5th Lon Inf Brig and two to H.Qrs 6th Lon Inf Brig on 28th aaa they will be placed in position in supporting points only and NOT in front line aaa acknowledge aaa addressed 4th repeated 5th and 6th Lon Inf Brigs

[Co to A d Q,
  9.35 hrs]

From: Lon Div
Time: 8.50 pm

"A" Form.
Army Form C. 2121

MESSAGES AND SIGNALS.   No. of Message_____

Prefix ___ Code ___ m	Words	Charge	This message is on a/c of:	Recd. at ___ m.
Office of Origin and Service Instructions	Sent		_____ Service.	Date ___
	At ___ m			From ___
	To ___			
	By ___		(Signature of "Franking Officer.")	By ___

TO { 1st Corps
2d Div

| Sender's Number. | Day of Month. | In reply to Number | AAA |
| G.B.348 | 27th | | |

In accordance with verbal permission have ordered machine gun detachments of 4th Lon Inf Brig to join 5th and 6th Lon Inf Brig on 28th ava addressed first corps repeated 2d Div

From Lon Div
Place
Time 7.50 pm

The above may be forwarded as now corrected.   (Z)

"A" Form.
Army Form C. 2121.

MESSAGES AND SIGNALS.

No. of Message _____

Prefix _____ Code _____ m. Words | Charge   This message is on a/c of: Recd. at _____ m.
Office of Origin and Service Instructions   Date _____
                                    Sent   Service   From _____
                                    At _____ m.
                                    To _____
                                    By _____   (Signature of "Franking Officer.")   By _____

TO { 1st Corps

Sender's Number.	Day of Month.	In reply to Number	AAA
GB 354	27th		

Reference verbal conversation today should
be glad of four machine guns from
motor machine gun battery for use in
front line area. Those of 4th London Inf Brig
will be used in supporting points

From: London Div
Place:
Time: 10.55 pm

"A" Form.
Army Form C. 2121.

MESSAGES AND SIGNALS.

No. of Message _____

Prefix	Code	m.	Words	Charge	This message is on a/c of:	Recd. at _____ m.
Office of Origin and Service Instructions			Sent			Date _____
			At _____ m.		_____ Service.	From _____
			To _____			By _____
			By _____		(Signature of "Franking Officer.")	

TO { 5th Lon Inf Brig
6th Lon Inf Brig

| Sender's Number. | Day of Month. | In reply to Number | AAA |
| G.B 35-5- | 27th | | |

Ref C/111 aaa Rendezvous for Divisional Reserve Bat'ns in case of their being ordered to be moved from quarters on an emergency will be as follows aaa Battalion of fifth Lon Inf Brig rendezvous GORRE with Hd'Qrs at GORRE Church aaa Battalion of sixth Lon Inf Brig rendezvous LE TOURET with Hd'Qrs at Cross Roads LE TOURET aaa Actual places of assembly under cover and routes to be selected and these will be communicated to and reconnoitred by relieving battalions aaa Time which would be taken to reach rendezvous from billets after receipt of order to move to be reported aaa These battalions will be ready to move at two hours notice but working parties would move direct to rendezvous without returning to billets aaa Communicate and acknowledge aaa Addressed

From	5th and 6th Lon Inf Brigs		PRIORITY
Place	Lon: Div		
Time	10.55 pm		

The above may be forwarded as now corrected. (Z)

Censor.   Signature of Addressee or person authorised to telegraph in his name.

* This line should be erased if not required.

"C" Form (Duplicate). Army Form C. 2123
MESSAGES AND SIGNALS.

Office Stamp: Y 28. IV. 15. LB ARMY TELEGRAPHS

Handed in at .... Office ...27.. m Received 1.54 m

TO

Sender's Number	Day of Month	In reply to Number	AAA
BM 441	28	GS 355	AAA

Time required by battn in divisional reserve to reach rendezvous from billets taken over this afternoon as follows aaa Two companies one hour aaa One Company One and a half hours aaa One Company One and three quarters of an hour after receipt of notice to move aaa

LP/802
6·10 PM (receipt)

FROM
PLACE & TIME   Sixth Corps Inf Bde
                 1.40 pm

O.C. 23rd Bn.

Forwarded for your information and
return – on the whole the reports are very
satisfactory
             H.E. Trevor Major
26.4.15.   Bgde 6th London Inf Bde

H.Q.
6th London Bde

Noted & Returned –

        John E Thornhill Capt Act
      OrCmg 23 Bn London R.
28/4/15

Headquarters
    London Division.

    Returned please.

                        csdWilloughby
                    Brigadier General comdg
                    6th Lon Inf Bde.

28. 4. 15.

Secret

To H.Q.,
　　London Division.

(1) I have this morning finished looking at the wire in the Festubert zone. I do not consider that it would be possible to effectively cut wire from the position at present occupied by the guns.

(2) I am of opinion that the wire could be cut near S.26.b.8.8. from a position near X.23.d.4.4. I would recommend that one gun of the 15th.Lon.Battery be sent to this place and that 20 rounds be allowed for the purpose of registering and seeing what result there may be.

(3) I have this afternoon visited the O.C.,34th.Bde.R.F.A. and have discussed with him and the G.O.C.R.A. 2nd.Division the best arrangements for cutting wire in C.1. and the southern portion of C.2. A new gun position will be reconnoitred for this purpose and I will report further as soon as this has been done.

(4) As regards the other zones, the GIVENCHY zone is practically impossible to deal with, and as far as GUINCHY is concerned a demonstration could be made by shooting at the wire (which would no doubt have some effect) without shifting the present position of the guns.

Brigadier-General,
Comdg.Lon.Divl.Arty.

DIVISIONAL ARTILLERY,
2nd LONDON DIVISION T.F.
B.M./690.
No.
28/4/15.

SECRET.

Copy No. 20

Amendments to :-

Lon.Div. Secret Memo No.G/111, dated 26th April, 1915,

****

Page 2, paragraph 5 (ii), line 8. Dele from "The place of deployment ...." to end of (ii), and substitute:-

"These reserves will be assembled in close proximity to the supporting line, viz - LE PLANTIN - FESTUBERT - RUE DE L'EPINETTE. From these positions, the exact site of which will be selected by Infantry Brigade Commanders, the Brigade Reserves are available to complete the action of local counterstrokes or, in case of extreme necessity should the enemy break through the line in strength, to occupy this supporting line which they would hold at all costs."

Paragraph 5 (iii). Dele whole para and substitute :-

"Divisional Reserves are maintained under the orders of the Divisional Commander for the purpose of a general counter attack in force in whichever section he may select. They are billeted some way back in order to ensure complete rest, but have rendezvous appointed to which they would move on receipt of orders. These rendezvous are known to Infantry Brigade Commanders. The G.O.C. has authorised Inf.Bde.Commanders to use the battalions of the Divisional Reserve without further reference in case of extreme necessity. They would report their action."

****

1st Division

The above amendments to Lon.Div.Secret Memo No.G/111, dated 26th April 1915, are forwarded for your information.   Kindly acknowledge receipt.

H.R. Hunt

No.G/111/2

29th April 1915.

Captain,
General Staff
for Major General
Commanding London Divn.

TACTICAL PROGRESS REPORT OF LONDON DIVISION
up to Noon 28th April, 1915.

OPERATIONS.   1.   Enemy shelled D1 and neighbourhood of BUR
                        DU BOIS and RUE DE L'EPINETTE at intervals
                        without effect.

WORK.   2.   C1 - New Breastworks in Front Line strengthened
                        throughout and positions made for firing fixed
                        rifles.

                        C2 - Parapet of Front Line strengthened and
                        raised.

                        D1 - Work continued on Communication trenches.
                        Breastwork reconstructed generally and work
                        carried out on parados where required. Damage
                        done to dug-outs and parapets repaired.

INFORMATION.   Hostile parties seen carrying planks between
                        H8 and H2, but no further work observed at those
                        points.

                        A little work done in S 28 b and in the enemy's
                        breastworks just North of RUE CAILLOUX.

                        Considerable work was done during the night
                        27th/28th on breastwork near P15 and on Northern
                        Communication Breastworks to East of this point.
                        This communication breastwork is now nearly
                        completed and a small gap only remains.

                        There is a deep re-entrant into the German
                        breastwork near the road East of P5. One side
                        of this faces North East and is partly formed of
                        brick. This point enfilades the front of the
                        breastwork to the North. There is a large hole
                        in it presumably for a Machine Gun. Germans
                        planted bushes in front of this during night of
                        27th/28th.

                                          Signed. B.BURNETT HITCHCOCK.
                                                             Major
                        L.D. G/61/8   for Major General,
                                             Commanding London Division.

"A" Form.
Army Form C. 2121.

MESSAGES AND SIGNALS.

No. of Message_____

Prefix	Code	m.	Words	Charge	This message is on a/c of:	Recd. at _____ m.
Office of Origin and Service Instructions			Sent		_____ Service.	Date _____
			At ____ m.			From _____
			To ____		(Signature of "Franking Officer.")	By _____

TO
4th Lon Inf Brig
5th Lon Inf Brig
6th Lon Inf Brig

Sender's Number	Day of Month	In reply to Number	AAA
CB 376	29th		

The detachments with gun machine guns will be relieved by other detachments from their own units every forty eight hours aaa acknowledge aaa addressed 4th Lon Inf Brig repeated fifth and sixth Lon Inf Brigs

From   Lon Div
Place
Time   8.50 am

"A" Form. Army Form C. 2121.

MESSAGES AND SIGNALS.   No. of Message_____

Prefix____ Code____ m.	Words	Charge	This message is on a/c of:	Recd. at_____ m.
Office of Origin and Service Instructions				Date_____
_____	Sent		_____Service.	From_____
_____	At____m. To____ By____		(Signature of "Franking Officer.")	By_____

TO { 5th Lon Inf Brig
     6th Lon Inf Brig

Sender's Number.	Day of Month.	In reply to Number	AAA
CB.377	Twenty-nine		

The Machine guns of Battalion in Divisional Reserve will be with the battalion and NOT included in the defence arrangements aaa Selfridge aaa addressed fifth and sixth Lon Inf Brigs

From Lon Div
Place
Time 9.45 am

"A" Form.
MESSAGES AND SIGNALS.
Army Form C. 2121.

Prefix	Code	m.	Words	Charge	This message is on a/c of:	Recd. at	m.
Office of Origin and Service Instructions.			Sent		Service.	Date	
			At	m.		From	
	-		To			By	
			By		(Signature of "Franking Officer.")		

TO	Edwards	Horse		
	Lon.	Div.	Cyclists	

Sender's Number.	Day of Month.	In reply to Number	AAA
G.H.378	29th		

The Rendezvous for Divisional Mounted Troops in Divl. Reserve is LA MOTTE Square X 26 c. with Headquarters at the Chapel at the Cross Roads F1 b AAA Routes will be reconnoitred at once and you will report how long it would take your command to reach this rendezvous calculated from time of marching off from present quarters AAA You will also reconnoitre lines of approach from the rendezvous towards either section of the defence AAA Acknowledge AAA Addressed Edwards Horse and Cyclists AAA

From Lon Div.
Place
Time 10.15 a.m.

H.R. Hunt Capt G.S.

"A" Form. Army Form C. 2121.
MESSAGES AND SIGNALS.

TO	LON	DIV		

Sender's Number.	Day of Month.	In reply to Number	AAA
C 203	29	G.H 378	

Approximate	time	it	would	take
LON	CYCLISTS	move	from	present
quarters	to	rendezvous	for	Divisional
Mounted	Troops	in	Divl	Reserve
is	half	an	hour	AAA

LO/440
8.5 pm

From: LON CYCLISTS
Place:
Time: 7.45 pm

SECRET.

2ND. LONDON DIVISION.

BILLETS OCCUPIED BY UNITS ON NIGHT OF 29TH. APRIL, 1915.

```
Divisional Hd.Qrs. .. .. .. .. .. .. BETHUNE.

4th. London Infantry Bde.
    Headquarters. .. .. .. .. .. .. LABEUVRIERE.
    6th. Bn. London Regt. .. .. .. .. LAPUGNOY.
    7th.   -"-    -"- .. .. .. .. LAPUGNOY.
    8th.   -"-    -"- .. .. .. .. LABEUVRIERE.
    15th.  -"-    -"- .. .. .. .. LABEUVRIERE.

5th. London Infantry Bde.
    Headquarters. .. .. .. .. .. .. LOISNE.
    17th. Bn. London Regt. .. .. .. ) 2 Battalions in trenches.
    18th.  -"-    -"- .. .. .. .. ) 1 Battn. GORRE & TUNINGFORK.
    19th.  -"-    -"- .. .. .. .. ) 1 Battn. GORRE & ESSARS.
    20th.  -"-    -"- .. .. .. .. )

6th. London Infantry Bde.
    Headquarters. .. .. .. .. .. .. Chateau de RAUX.
    21st. Bn. London Regt. .. .. .. ) 2 Battalions in trenches.
    22nd.  -"-    -"- .. .. .. .. ) 1 Battn. LE TOURET & RUE de
    23rd.  -"-    -"- .. .. .. .. ) L'EPINETTE.
    24th.  -"-    -"- .. .. .. .. ) 1 Battn. ESSARS, LES FACONS &
                                    ) W.24.c.

Divisional Mounted Troops.
    "C" Squadron, King Edward's Horse. .. FONTENELLE FARM.
    Divisional Cyclist Company. .. .. .. BETHUNE.

Divisional Artillery.
    Headquarters. .. .. .. .. .. .. BETHUNE.
    5th. London Brigade R.F.A. .. .. .. LE HAMEL.
    6th. London Brigade R.F.A. .. .. .. LOISNE.
    7th. London Brigade R.F.A. .. .. .. CAMBRIN.
    8th. London (How) Brigade R.F.A. .. Attached 1st. Division.
    Divisional Ammunition Column. .. .. ANNEZIN.

Divisional Engineers.
    Headquarters. .. .. .. .. .. .. BETHUNE.
    3rd. London Field Company R.E. .. .. GORRE.
    4th. London Field Company R.E. .. .. LES CLAUGMES & LES FACONS.

Divisional Train.
    Headquarters. .. .. .. .. .. .. BETHUNE.
    Hd.Qr. Company Train. .. .. .. .. BETHUNE.
    Nos. 2, 3, & 4 Cos. Train .. .. .. BETHUNE.
    Divisional Supply Column. .. .. .. LOZINGHEM.

R.A.M.C.
    4th. London Field Ambulance .. .. LABEUVRIERE.
    5th. London Field Ambulance .. .. ALLOUAGNE.
    6th. London Field Ambulance .. .. BETHUNE.
    Motor Ambulance Workshop .. .. .. BETHUNE.
    Divisional Sanitary Section. .. .. BETHUNE.

Mobile Veterinary Section. .. .. .. BETHUNE.
```

TACTICAL PROGRESS REPORT OF LONDON DIVISION

UP TO NOON 29th APRIL 1915.

OPERATIONS. 1. Our Artillery fired on German working party near M.3.

The enemy's Artillery fired a few high explosive shell on our trench opposite J.1 and J.2 and appeared to be registering this point.

WORK. 2. C.1. Communication trench to Work A commenced. Work continued on new breastwork. Considerable work carried out on wire.

C.2. Front breastwork and communications improved.

D.1. Communication trench from Deadcow Farm to Crooked Tree continued.
Several yards of parados in front line completed.
Old dug outs removed from front line trenches and new ones commenced.

INFORMATION. 3. Three wooden hutches with sliding doors 2 feet high and 3 feet wide seen about 15 yards in front of enemy's line at M.3. One of these hutches was moved slightly Southwards during the day. They are thought to be portable snipers posts. Further information has been asked for.
Wires on low poles near Work K appear to be ordinary telegraph wires and lead to the enemy's fire breastwork and to his communication breastwork.
Machine guns located S.20.b.7.5. and near P.2.

In report for period ending 12 noon 28th inst. in the third paragraph of subheading INFORMATION, for "PJ5." read "M.3."

WATER LEVEL. 4. The water level fell ½ inch in C. and 2 inches in D.1. (b).

        (Sgd.)   Wm. THWAITES, Lt.Colonel,

                     for/ Major General,

L.D. G/51/6.   Commanding London Division.

Headquarters
Lahore Division

No. G/111/2, df. 29.4.15.
Secret letter (Copy 16) containing
amendments to Lahore Division Secret Memo
No. G/111 dated 26th April 1915 received.

A.H.Kenney Col.
29.4.15. C.O. Lah. Dn.

6th Lon. Inf. Bde.

Please note that on the night 2/3rd May the 1st Guards Brigade will relieve the 2nd Infantry Brigade in sub-sections D.2 and D.3 from CHOCOLAT MENIER CORNER (inclusive) to the ORCHARD REDOUBT (exclusive).

                                              Major,
                                       General Staff,
30th April 1915.   London Division.

5th Lon. Inf. Bde.

Please note that the 5th Infantry Brigade will take over Section "A" (CUINCHY) from 6th Infantry Brigade on the night of 3rd/4th May under arrangements to be made direct between the Brigade Commanders concerned.

                                              Major,
                                       General Staff,
30th April 1915.   London Division.

SECRET

2/London Division

1st ARMY General STAFF.
No: G.S. 73(a)
Date: 30/4/15

4

CONFERENCE, 1st ARMY, 27th April, AT BETHUNE.

1. The conference was attended by all Corps and Divisional Commanders, with their S.G.S.Os. and C.R.As. (except the Lahore and 2nd London Divisions) and by the Commanders of Nos. 1 and 2 Groups, H.A.R.

2. The G.O.C. laid stress on the following points :-

   (a). The three main phases of attack are as follows :-

   First   - 1st Corps and Indian Corps to secure the line RUE DU MARAIS - LORGIES - LIGNY-le-PETIT. 4th Corps to secure FROMELLES and the FROMELLES - AUBERS road.

   Secondly - The Indian Corps and the 4th Corps to secure the high ground about LIGNY-le-GRAND and LA CLIQUETERIE FARM.

   Thirdly   - The advance on DON.

   (b). The artillery should be disposed with this object. (see special instructions to artillery, copy attached).

   (c). All plans are to be made with the object of getting right on and continuing the advance.

   (d). Fresh troops to be always at hand to fill up gaps and to push on the forward movement when troops in front are fatigued or held up.
   In this connection it was pointed out that this does not mean reinforcing with more troops a line which is held up and is already sufficiently strong. (See 1st Army Memorandum, G.S. 73 (a) of 13th inst., Paper 'B', paragraph 2.)

3. Attention was drawn to the possibility of a gap occurring between the left of 1st Corps and the right of Indian Corps. The line of demarkation was clear (i.e. the DISTILLERY - the FERME-du-BIEZ, and the FERME-du-BIEZ - LIGNY-le-PETIT - LIGNY-le-GRAND road inclusive assigned to the Indian Corps), and it was pointed out that, in the event of a gap occurring, Brigadiers and Battalion Commanders must at once send forward troops to fill it without waiting for orders from behind. There will often be, on such occasions, neither the time nor the possibility of communicating with higher authority, and commanders, having been told the intention and the plan, must

act

2.

act on their own initiative. (See 1st Army Memorandum G.S. 73 (a) of 13th inst., Paper 'B', paragraph 2).

4. The general principles and method of attack were discussed, viz:- the systematic seizure and occupation of localities in as rapid a sequence as possible, definite objectives, as far as possible, being assigned to definite battalions or companies. The duty of placing captured localities in a state of defence, of dealing with prisoners, etc., is to be assigned to definite parties pushed up from the rear, and not to parties dropped by troops pushing on the attack. (See 1st Army Memorandum G.S. 73 (a) of 13th inst., Paper 'B', paragraph 3.)

5. The method of dealing with the BOIS DU BIEZ was discussed. It was pointed out that the seizure of this wood and the capture or masking of LA RUSSIE was a necessary adjunct to the advance on LIGNY-le-GRAND. The Infantry Brigade charged with the advance on LIGNY-le-Grand must have its left flank protected, but, owing to the danger of being diverted from its objective, should not be required to detach troops into the wood. The task of dealing with the BOIS DU BIEZ and LA RUSSIE must, therefore, be assigned to troops specially detailed for this purpose.

6. The importance of pushing forward light guns or mortars with the infantry was noted. Instructions on the formation of the Mortar Batteries have been issued, and it is hoped that mortars will arrive in sufficient numbers for a battery to be with each Infantry Brigade. It was pointed out that these batteries, though in some cases manned by artillery personnel, were an infantry

weapon

weapon under the orders of the Infantry Commander, and were not artillery.

7. The attention of G.Os.C., 4th and Indian Corps was drawn to the strength of the German forces likely to be in the area NEUVE CHAPELLE - AUBERS - FAUQUISSART (4,000 to 5,000 men and about 12 to 20 guns) should the attack succeed as arranged. The method of dealing with this force is to be specially provided for in the plans of Divisions.

8. The G.O.C. drew attention to the strength of Infantry Brigades. Considering the size of Infantry Brigades, as at present constituted, it is advisable that each Brigadier should have a small detachment of mounted men at his disposal.

R. Butler.
Brigadier-General

30th April, 1915.   General Staff, 1st Army.

"A" Form. Army Form C. 2121.
MESSAGES AND SIGNALS.

TO: LONDON DIVISION

Sender's Number: SC.125
Day of Month: 30
AAA

The following message has been received and is forwarded for your information AAA begins 4 London Battery observing officer reports hosepipes in following positions enemys front breastwork AAA S/15B/9-7 AAA S/15B/8-6 where communication trench runs into breastwork at R6 AAA midway between R2 and R6 AAA no fumes AAA Reference maps 1/20,000 and 1/5000 ends AAA

D.4.57
3.28 pm

From: LONDON DIVN ARTY
Time: 3.15 pm

Harold Hall, Major

"A" Form. Army Form C. 2121

MESSAGES AND SIGNALS.   No. of Message_____

Prefix	Code	m	Words	Charge	This message is on a/c of:	Recd. at	m
Office of Origin and Service Instructions			Sent			Date	
			At	m	_____ Service.	From	
			To			By	
			By		(Signature of "Franking Officer.")		

TO	1st Corps		
	1st Div		
	Sixth Lon Inf Bde		

Sender's Number.	Day of Month.	In reply to Number	AAA
SB.396	Thirtieth		

14th Lon Battery Observing Officer reports hosepipes in following positions enemy's front breastwork AAA S.15/B/9.7 AAA S.15/B/8.6 where communication trench runs into breastwork at R.6 AAA Midway between R.2 and R.6 AAA no fumes AAA Reference maps 1/20,000 and 1/5000 AAA Addressed 1st Corps repeated 1st Division and Sixth Lon Inf Bde

From: Lon Div
Place:
Time: 3.52 pm

"C" Form (Duplicate).   Army Form C. 2123.
MESSAGES AND SIGNALS.   No. of Message_____

Service Instructions.

Handed in at _____ Office ___ m. Received 4.19 m.

TO

Sender's Number	Day of Month	In reply to Number	AAA
G.835	30.		

Destroy hosepipes seen by 14th London batty forthwith

FROM
PLACE & TIME 1st Corps

"A" Form.   Army Form C. 2121.
MESSAGES AND SIGNALS.   No. of Message_____

Prefix	Code	m	Words	Charge	This message is on a/c of:	Recd. at____m
Office of Origin and Service Instructions			Sent		_____Service.	Date_____
			At____m			From_____
			To			
			By	(Signature of "Franking Officer.")		By_____

TO { Lon. Div. Engrs
     Fifth Lon Inf Bde
     Sixth Lon Inf Bde

Sender's Number.	Day of Month.	In reply to Number	AAA
GB 397	Thirtieth		

From midnight on 3rd/4th May the 5th Field Company RE will be available for work on Sections "C" and "D.1" AAA The C.R.E. will decide in consultation with Fifth and Sixth Lon Inf Bdes how the company can be employed to best advantage AAA Addressed Lon Div Engrs repeated Fifth and Sixth Lon Inf Bdes

From Lon Div.
Place
Time 4.20 p.m.

"A" Form.
MESSAGES AND SIGNALS.

Army Form C. 2121.
No. of Message _____

Prefix	Code	m.	Words	Charge	This message is on a/c of:	Recd. at	m.
Office of Origin and Service Instructions.			Sent			Date	
			At	m.		From	
			To		Service.		
			By		(Signature of "Franking Officer.")	By	

TO { Lon. Div. Arty
     1st Division
     Sixth Lon Inf Bde

Sender's Number.	Day of Month	In reply to Number	
* G B 399	Thirtieth		A A A

1st Corps orders destruction of hose pipes forthwith AAA Addressed Lon Div Arty Repeated 1st Div and Sixth Lon Inf Bde

From: Lon Div
Place:
Time: 4.23 pm

The above may be forwarded as now corrected. (Z)

Censor. Signature of Addressor or person authorised to telegraph in his name.

* This line should be erased if not required.

"C" Form (Duplicate).   Army Form C. 2123.

MESSAGES AND SIGNALS.

No. of Message _____

Service Instructions.

Handed in at _____ Office ____ m. Received ____ m.

TO _____ Div.

Sender's Number	Day of Month	In reply to Number	AAA
G837	21		
Reference my G835 repeated 1st			
Div.			
		4D/462	
		4 42 pm	X

FROM 1st Corps
PLACE & TIME 4.30 pm

"A" Form.   Army Form C. 2121.
MESSAGES AND SIGNALS.   No. of Message_____

Prefix____ Code____ m.	Words	Charge	This message is on a/c of:	Recd. at_____ m.
Office of Origin and Service Instructions.				Date_____
	Sent		_____Service.	From_____
	At_____ m.			
	To_____			By_____
	By_____	(Signature of "Franking Officer.")		

| TO | Lon | Div | Engrs | |
| | Sixth | Lon | Inf | Bde |

| Sender's Number. | Day of Month. | In reply to Number | AAA |
| G.B./400 | Thirtieth | | |

Reference	1st Corps	~~dated~~ G.767	the
2nd	Division	will	detail	a
working	party	to	reconstruct	work
E.3	in	"D.1"	section	on
any	night	next	week	suitable
to	G.O.C.	Sixth	Lon	Inf
Bde	AAA	He	will	kindly
report	date	decided	on	with
least	possible	delay	AAA	5th
Field	Coy.	R.E.	will superintend	
the	work	AAA	Addressed	Lon
Div.	Engrs	and	Sixth	Lon
Inf	Bde			
				X

From	Lon Div.	
Place		Burnett Mitchell
Time	5 pm	Major

The above may be forwarded as now corrected.   (Z)
Censor.   Signature of Addressor or person authorised to telegraph in his name.
* This line should be erased if not required.

TACTICAL PROGRESS REPORT OF LONDON DIVISION

up to noon 30th April 1915.

OPERATIONS.   1.   Our Artillery fired on Machine Gun emplacement near
P.2 making a considerable breach in the parapet close
to the emplacement.

WORK.   2.   C.1 and 2.   Breastwork in front line improved.

D.1.   General improvements to parapet and traverses
carried out.
Construction of S.A.A. and bomb houses commenced.
Work on communication trenches continued.

INFORMATION.   3.   Enemy opposite D.1 appear to be sniping at night from
their front breastworks.   Observers state that no flashes
were observed from positions in rear.

Transport was heard last night near road junction N.8.

An officer well acquainted with German carried out two
reconnaissances as far as the German wire opposite C.2.
He reports that the troops occupying this section during
the night of 29th/30th were Bavarians and that during the
night of 28th/29th another dialect was spoken which he
could not identify.

(Sd) Wm.THWAITES, Lt.Colonel,

for/   Major General,

L.D. G/S1/7.   Commanding London Division.